AMMO+GRACE

THE DEVOTIONAL

COTE ANNE

TABLE OF CONTENTS

Foreword ix

Day 1 1
Day 2 3
Day 3 5
Day 4 8
Day 5 10
Day 6 12
Day 7 14
Day 8 17
Day 9 19
Day 10 22
Day 11 24
Day 12 27
Day 13 30
Day 14 32
Day 15 34
Day 16 37
Day 17 39
Day 18 42
Day 19 44
Day 20 47
Day 21 50
Day 22 53
Day 23 56
Day 24 58
Day 25 61
Day 26 64
Day 27 66
Day 28 69
Day 29 72
Day 30 75
Day 31 78

Day 32 81
Day 33 83
Day 34 86
Day 35 89
Day 36 92
Day 37 95
Day 38 97
Day 39 100
Day 40 103
Day 41 106
Day 42 109
Day 43 111
Day 44 114
Day 45 117
Day 46 120
Day 47 123
Day 48 125
Day 49 128
Day 50 131

Notes 135
About the Author 137

Cover Artwork by BMonte Designs LLC

DEDICATION

To my police officer, without whom I would not be a police wife. Thank you for building a beautiful life with me and being my person.

FOREWORD

Yay! I'm so glad you're here! This devotional has been on my heart for years. At the end of 2018, I felt the Lord's nudging turn into a much stronger push, and knew I needed to answer the call. Enter ... this book! Whether you've been loving an officer for decades or just begun the journey, whether you're deep in your faith or still testing the waters-you are welcomed here with open arms.

I hope these fifty days of devotionals bring you closer to God and to your officer. May these words and verses help you embrace your role as the heart behind the badge and bring you comfort and encouragement in this crazy blue life. I hope that sharing my heart helps make this wild ride feel less lonely and more relatable for you.

Now grab some coffee and comfy pants-let's devo!

REVIEWS FOR AMMO+GRACE: THE DEVOTIONAL

Ammo+Grace: The Devotional is a great devotional for those of us learning how to live out our trust in God as our daily lives are challenged by fear. As Police Spouses we can live our lives with joy and hope amidst all of the voices that clamor for our peace. Make this book a part of your worship and strengthen your relationship with Jesus. I certainly have.

-Chaplain Lisa Lerner
Founder of Bless The Badge Ministries

Ammo+Grace: The Devotional is a book written through experience as a police wife and finding God's grace amidst it all. You will find that the author is transparent and genuine, leaving the reader with so much encouragement. The use of scripture to back up the message given in each devotion is perfect for life application. This is a book that will provide hope for any law enforcement wife.

-Allison P. Uribe
Founder of Wives on Duty Ministries

DAY 1

SPECIAL DAYS ARE THE DAYS WE MAKE SPECIAL

"For where two or three gather in my name, there am I with them."
MATTHEW 18:20

Draw near to God and He will draw near to you.
JAMES 4:8 NKJV

One of the first things that comes to mind when I think of blue life is the difficult shift work, which of course means the missed holidays and nonexistent weekends. It's a hard adjustment for families who are used to working Monday through Friday and having Christmas and Thanksgiving and all the "traditional holidays" off. Since we were young children in school, we've been used to the routine of getting weekends and holidays off, and leaving home in the morning and returning around dark. Police life, however, turns all of that upside down (and backward and inside out).

But the thing is, holidays aren't just the days marked on

the calendar. Special days are the days that we make special.

I'll be the first to admit that our first few "adjusted" holidays were tough. It felt so odd to wake up on Christmas morning alone, or to have Thanksgiving dinner a week early. I soon realized, however, that all the important elements were still there on the days we celebrated: the family, the laughter, the music, the food, and the prayer. Those things don't change depending on which day the holiday falls on the calendar, and they certainly don't change depending on the day your family chooses to celebrate.

Matthew 18 tells us that when a few of us gather in the Lord's name, He is there. It doesn't say "if you gather on December 25" or "but only if you gather on Easter Sunday." No. It says *any* time.

Police families are amazing at being flexible—because we have to be! I've learned that it's a hidden blessing to celebrate holidays on days that work for our family because it forces us to focus on the things that really matter, and that never includes the date on the calendar.

PRAYER

Lord, we are so grateful that You're with us no matter our circumstances. Regardless of the day we're celebrating a special holiday, You are present with us. Please remind us what the true meaning of holidays are and that the things that make holidays special aren't dependent on the date they are celebrated.

DAY 2

MY POWER IS MADE PERFECT IN WEAKNESS

But he said to me, "My grace is sufficient for you, for my power is made perfect in weakness." Therefore I will boast all the more gladly about my weaknesses, so that Christ's power may rest on me.

2 CORINTHIANS 12:9

It may seem odd to highlight weakness in a book that talks about being a LEOW. Doesn't the world tell us that weakness is bad, and that we need to be strong—for ourselves, for our spouses, and for our families? Well, yes. Yes and no.

I know you're strong, because you wouldn't be in the role of LEOW if you weren't. You know that saying "God made the strongest women police wives"? It's true! But the truth is, we can't be strong 100 percent of the time. Luckily for us, God says that's okay—that He works best with those who reach out to Him in their times of weakness. His grace covers our flaws, and His power overcomes our weakness.

Because we're only human, we're bound to fall short sometimes. Maybe it's falling short with the housekeeping; the laundry is overflowing, you forgot to buy more Clorox wipes, and the garage has stacks of boxes you've been meaning to go through (since you moved in two years ago). Maybe it's at work, where you try and try to get ahead but this week the emails just keep pouring in, the to-do list is pages long, and sticky notes cover your entire computer monitor. Maybe it's in your marriage; your patience is simply thinner this week, you've become annoyed at your spouse's normal quirks, and your mouth keeps opening before you can filter the things that spill out.

We all fall short sometimes, but when we reach out to God, He can help us cover those shortcomings. We're not expected to be perfect, but we are expected to be pursuing Him. When we're weak, He remains strong. When we fall short, His grace still remains. Isn't that encouraging? In which ways is God's strength most evident in your life?

PRAYER

Lord, today I ask for Your grace and power. You've created me intricately and wonderfully, and with You I lack nothing. Please remind me of this when I second-guess myself, when I feel weak, and when I need a little encouragement. I pray that You'll use me as a rock for my officer and my family in times of weakness, a rock that rests on the firmest of all foundations—You. Remind us to turn to You when we're feeling weak or defeated so that we may be reminded of Your loving grace.

DAY 3

WORK FOR THE LORD RATHER THAN PEOPLE

Work willingly at whatever you do, as though you were working for the Lord rather than for people.
Colossians 3:23 NLT

Work with enthusiasm, as though you were working for the Lord rather than for people.
Ephesians 6:7 NLT

I can't speak for every officer, but I truly believe that most entered their profession wanting to make a difference. It certainly wasn't for the money or recognition—especially in the current anti-police climate. We were put on this earth to be God's hands and feet, and this role can look different for each of us. I see God's will acted out so visibly each time I see a story on the news about an officer helping a family, when I hear my officer talk about a time he showed a citizen grace, or when I drive by a trooper helping someone change a flat tire on the side of the road.

All these stories are examples of working for the Lord. We know that good deeds don't always get noticed. We know that the calls our officers go on don't always end well. We know that the people they're trying to help don't always want to be helped. We know that officers rarely make the news for positive calls, but always end up on YouTube when something negative happens. And still, our officers serve. Still, they show up.

The story in 2 Chronicles 31 describes the reign of King Solomon and the split of Israel into two kingdoms. King Hezekiah organizes offerings and sacrifices that the people all give. Not only do they give, but they give *happily*. Through it all King Hezekiah keeps seeking God and His will, and because of this, he is successful.

> In this way, King Hezekiah handled the distribution throughout all Judah, doing what was pleasing and good in the sight of the LORD his God. In all that he did in the service of the Temple of God and in his efforts to follow God's laws and commands, Hezekiah sought his God wholeheartedly. As a result, he was very successful.
>
> 2 CHRONICLES 31:20–21 NLT

We might not always see the fruit of our labor. Our officers will not always be thanked for their work, and they will often get discouraged. But when we remind ourselves that we're working for the Lord and not for man, we're able to remember why we're here and what our purpose is. And when we work in accordance with God's will, we're promised that we will be successful.

PRAYER

Lord, we are fortunate to work for a "boss" who is so forgiving and fruitful and just. When we get tired, please remind us of Your purpose. When we question why things are going the way they are—or aren't going the way we hoped—speak into our lives. Remind us of Your presence and that You have a plan. We will tire when working for man but prosper when we work for You.

DAY 4

CLING TO WHAT IS GOOD

Love must be sincere. Detest what is evil and cling to what is good.
ROMANS 12:9 BSB

But test everything that is said. Hold on to what is good.
1 THESSALONIANS 5:21 NLT

Until I became a police wife, I didn't know how absolutely horrid the internet can be. Websites and social media can spew hate and lies faster than my fingers can scroll. It's easy to fall into the Enemy's trap and get wrapped up in the articles. It's easy to click and click and become enraged by the anti-police propaganda and the hateful comments popping up on the screen. It's hard to remember to cling to the good.

I work as a family therapist with high-risk families, and sometimes our progress (or lack of) can be discouraging. My consultant often reminds me to "feast on crumbs." In other words, to focus on the little victories. The small successes. The positives. Even if they're tiny, little, minuscule crumbs.

And isn't that true for life in general? We can be quickly swept away by the negativity, but when we fix our eyes on Jesus and the good He has placed in our lives, our attitudes begin to shift. They change. Maybe this tidbit of goodness is that perfectly brewed cup of coffee or your officer getting home five minutes early (or even on time!). Maybe it's getting your Amazon package just as you're about to leave for your holiday party or snagging the last parking spot at a busy store when you're in a hurry. Or maybe it's simply seeing another day and getting to kiss your officer when he makes it home safely one more time.

What negativity to you feel yourself being drawn into that you need to take your eyes off of today? What crumbs of goodness can you replace them with? Whatever your "crumbs" may be, may you feast on them and the goodness that the Lord has created in your life.

PRAYER

Lord, in a world that is so broken, help me cling to what is good. In a world that tries so hard to make us believe the Enemy's lies, help me hold fast to Your truths. In a world that tries to convince me that I am broken, lacking, and incomplete, remind me that I am made perfectly in Your image. Remind me of the small victories I have each day. Remind me of the goodness You have placed in my life, and help me fix my eyes on that instead of the negative.

DAY 5

HER MOUTH SPEAKS WHAT FILLS HER

A good man brings good things out of the good stored up in his heart, and an evil man brings evil things out of the evil stored up in his heart. For the mouth speaks what the heart is full of.

LUKE 6:45

Create in me a pure heart, O God, and renew a steadfast spirit within me.

PSALM 51:10

Take delight in the LORD, and He will give you the desires of your heart.

PSALM 37:4 NLT

Have you ever heard the tale of the spilled coffee? It declares that we don't spill coffee because someone bumped into us, or because it slipped out of our hands; we spill coffee because that's what's in our mug. If there was tea in the mug, we would spill tea instead. Whatever is in the mug, whether coffee or tea, comes out when the mug gets jostled or dropped.

Friends, the same is true of our heart. When we are bumped into or broken, what comes out? Is it kindness or anger? Is it bitterness or forgiveness?

Blue life offers us countless opportunities to shape our hearts. When a stranger makes a snide comment about our thin blue line shirt, will we respond with grace or rage? When our officer gets pulled away unexpectedly from holiday supper, will our hearts leak out understanding or bitterness? When a neighbor jokes about our "imaginary husband" (or ask if we got a divorce) will we laugh it off or lash out?

Our mouths speak what our hearts are full of, and our lives reflect our hearts. What will we fill our hearts and our lives with? What's filling your heart right now?

PRAYER

Lord, renew my heart. Create in me the heart that You want me to have. Help me be filled with kindness, grace, love, and praise. Help me respond to my officer with patience and love. Help me serve our family with a heart that longs for You. Help me respond to situations and trials in ways that You would, Lord. When I am broken, let Your presence seep out. When I am shaken, let Your Word pour out.

DAY 6

THIS HOME SERVES THE LORD

This home serves the Lord.
JOSHUA 24:15 (PARAPHRASE)

No weapon formed against us will prosper. This home is righteous.
ISAIAH 54:17 (PARAPHRASE)

We are covered by His wings. We have refuge. He is our shield. He is faithful.
PSALM 91:4 (PARAPHRASE)

This home is peaceful.
LUKE 10:5 (PARAPHRASE)

This home is righteous, and it will remain standing. It will flourish and not be destroyed. Its rooms are full of riches.
PROVERBS 14 (PARAPHRASE)

Our officers are constantly surrounded by negativity. They see, hear, smell, and feel things that are stressful and exhausting each and every time they go to work and walk their beat. We ourselves are exposed to this as well as everyday sin, because we live in a broken world. It's extra important, then, to maintain peace and safety in our homes.

It's important to me that I speak truths over our home on a daily basis. Before bed and during my nighttime routine of checking locks, loading Glocks, and setting alarms, I pray over our home and affirm the truths over our doors. In the morning during my quiet time, I sing (offkey, of course) the Lord's praises throughout our rooms.

The Enemy is not welcome in our home. Evil has no place here. Our home is to be a heavenly place of rest and comfort and a blessed relief after my officer has been in a warzone all day. It's to be a safe place to land after being out in the world and feeling attacked and targeted.

Y'all, God's Word is *powerful* and sometimes we forget that. We have been given these truths for a reason. When we proclaim them over our lives and our homes, it matters. Are you taking the time to proclaim truths over your home on a regular basis? What promises will you bless your home with today?

PRAYER

Lord, You have blessed our family with a beautiful and loving home, and for that we are so grateful. Let it be a place of comfort and rest. Let it be a place of safety and love. Let Your truths be spoken in our rooms and Your name be praised throughout our walls. Protect our home with Your covenant, and bless those who step inside.

DAY 7

WORSHIP

Praise the LORD! Praise God in his sanctuary; praise him in his mighty heaven! Praise him for his mighty works; praise his unequaled greatness! Praise him with a blast of the ram's horn; praise him with lyre and harp! Praise him with the tambourine and dancing; praise him with strings and flutes! Praise him with a clash of cymbals; praise him with loud clanging cymbals.

PSALM 150:1–6 NLT

Through Jesus, therefore, let us continually offer to God a sacrifice of praise—the fruit of lips that openly profess his name.

HEBREWS 13:15

"God is spirit, so those who worship him must worship in spirit and truth."

JOHN 4:24 NLT

When I think of worship, I immediately think of song. I think about standing in church with my arms held high or belting out Hillsong lyrics in my kitchen on a sunny Saturday morning.

But true worship also makes me think of kneeling by our bed, with my hands covering my tear streaked face, attempting to pray and failing to have a single word come out. I think of praising God through gritted teeth when I'm angry with His plan but know in my heart that it (and He) is still good. I think of anonymously paying for the car behind me in the coffee line and smiling kindly at the woman next to me pumping gas.

We worship God through songs of praise at church, but we also worship Him through our actions and the way we live our everyday lives. Sometimes that looks like hymns and prayer, and sometimes it looks like showing kindness and grace. I personally find it easier to worship when my life is going well, like after a fulfilling church service or a fun weekend with my family. I find it harder to worship when I'm struggling, like when we learn of a line-of-duty death or my officer gets called into work unexpectedly and we need to cancel our plans.

Our worship and praise, however, isn't based on our circumstances or our feelings. It's based on God—and He always remains faithful and steady. How are you choosing to praise God today?

PRAYER

Lord, You are always with me. You are always good. And You are always deserving of my praise. Thank you for giving me breath to worship You with. Thank you for giving me my officer's hands to hold as we praise You. Through song and prayer and action, let our family worship You day in and day out.

DAY 8

THE RIGHTEOUS ARE AS BOLD AS LIONS

The wicked run away when no one is chasing them, but the godly are as bold as lions.
PROVERBS 28:1 NLT

God blesses those who hunger and thirst for justice, for they will be satisfied.
MATTHEW 5:6 NLT

Righteousness and justice are the foundation of your throne; love and faithfulness go before you.
PSALM 89:14

As LEOWs (law enforcement officer wives) we're used to seeing the image of a lion used in blue support. We see them on tribute shirts, in memes, and on coffee cups. Not only are lions used as a symbol of strength and leadership but they're also referenced in the Bible, often used as metaphors for both the good and the bad.

I would be lying if I didn't tell you that I often think of *The Lion King* when I see those shirts and mugs. Even though *TLK* is technically a children's movie (but c'mon, it's a classic), I think we can gather some powerful lessons from it. In it, the lions are clear symbols of power—and isn't that true of our officers as well? They're also thrust into the spotlight to lead their pack, even when they feel unprepared or unworthy like Simba did. They're the main source of protection for their kingdom, in good times and bad. They are bold and they are righteous. They are lions.

This week I encourage you to appreciate your officer for the bold lion he is, while also realizing that his role doesn't come without cost. How blessed are we to have officers who care for those who care so little, and who pursue boldly when all else flee? This life is not always easy, but it is our calling.

PRAYER

Lord, thank you for giving me my own personal lion. You have created my officer with such bravery and boldness. Please forgive me if I don't recognize that enough. I ask that You protect him as he is off protecting the kingdom, and grant me peace of mind when he's away. I pray that You'll use my officer's lion heart as an example to people who don't know You, and that through his courage and loyalty they'll begin to see Your goodness and Your sacrifice.

DAY 9

PRAISE THE LORD WHO TRAINS HIS HANDS FOR BATTLE AND HIS FINGERS FOR WAR

Praise be to the LORD my Rock, who trains my hands for war, my fingers for battle. He is my loving God and my fortress, my stronghold and my deliverer, my shield, in whom I take refuge, who subdues peoples under me.
PSALM 144:1–2

The LORD is my rock, my fortress and my deliverer; my God is my rock, in whom I take refuge, my shield and the horn of my salvation, my stronghold.
PSALM 18:2

The wicked run away when no one is chasing them, but the godly are as bold as lions.
PROVERBS 28:1 NLT

I've always loved the book of Psalms and the messages it shares. Since becoming a LEOW, a few parts of this book have jumped out at me. In Psalm 18 we hear of David being beaten by Saul—I mean, viciously attacked—but the Lord drew him out of deep waters (v. 16) and rescued him from the cords of death that entangled him (v. 4). Now before you say anything, I get it. I get that this stuff is hard to think about. After that dark sentence, you might be wondering why I'm frightening you with talk of death and evil.

And you'd be right by wondering. That stuff is scary, and not exactly something that we like to discuss or marinate on. But the reality is our officers face peril each time they put on their uniforms. They arrive at dangerous situations all of the time; that's just how it is in their profession. Their job is extremely dangerous—and one that is especially trying in this day and age of anti-police culture. I used to get really stressed out about it, and to be honest, sometimes I still do. But I've realized there are a few things protecting my officer that make it easier not to worry as much.

First, he is well trained. All of those months at academy, all of those hours at training days, all of those bullets spent at the range, all the tools that sit on his duty belt—those things are all about preparing our officers to do their job, and to do it well. I also have faith in my officer's coworkers. I trust that his department is set up to take care of business and provide its officers with the tools they need to do their job as safely as possible. And I trust that God has His hand on my officer at all times.

Does this mean that nothing bad can happen to him? No. I wish that were the case, but it's not. But I do know that my officer will do everything in his power to do his job well and to come home to me at the end of the day. I also know that the Lord is watching over both of us and has our story already written. Our officers have been called to do a hard job, a dangerous job, and a thankless job, but they have not been called to it without preparation and protection.

PRAYER

Lord, You are strong and You are faithful. Thank you for helping prepare my officer for the tasks he faces every day. You have knit him together and specifically prepared his fingers for the battles he will face. You have created his hands to be capable of the wars he may see. And you have instilled a braveness and righteousness in his heart that allows him to carry out his calling each day. Thank you, God, for creating him this way.

DAY 10

WE ARE NOT GIVEN THE SPIRIT OF FEAR

For God has not given us a spirit of fear and timidity, but of power, love, and self-discipline.
2 TIMOTHY 1:7 NLT

There is no fear in love. But perfect love drives out fear, because fear has to do with punishment. The one who fears is not made perfect in love.
1 JOHN 4:18

Some days I can be a very fearful person. Sometimes that fear stirs up when my officer leaves for a shift, and sometimes it rears its ugly head when I wake up panicked in the middle of the night in an empty bed and wonder if he's okay. And sometimes that fear presents itself as worrisome thoughts that swirl around aimlessly in my head, or it shows up as anxious dreams that creep up on me in the night.

As scary and real as those thoughts are, they aren't coming from God. God has not given us the spirit of fear; that is coming straight from the Enemy. When we're having fearful thoughts, they aren't stemming from God and His truths. I encourage you to recognize this the next time fear sneaks its way into your life. Acknowledge that no matter the size of the fear, our God is bigger and those fears can be cast out.

Does this automatically make them less frightening or stressful? No, not always. Fears and worries are real, especially in this difficult life we live, walking the thin blue line together. However, I've found that when I take a second to fact check (e.g., ask myself, *Where are these thoughts coming from? Are they reasonable? Who is really in control?),* I begin to feel better. When I remind myself of whose I am and who is looking out for our family, I immediately feel encouraged. When I spend time in prayer or worship, those fears start to dissipate and the Holy Spirit in me strengthens.

The next time fear strikes, take a step back. Breathe. Pray. Ask where the thoughts are coming from. And know that the Lord is in control.

PRAYER

Lord, today I ask You to remind me of Your Spirit. It is full of grace and love and has no place for fear, for Your perfect love casts out all fear. When fearful thoughts sneak into my life, arm me with Your Word so that I might throw them back out to where they came from. When the Enemy tries to trick me with fear, remind me of Your goodness and faithfulness. Be with me, Lord, armed with Your Word and feet planted solid in my faith so I will always recognize that the fearful thoughts are not coming from You, but can be overcome by You.

DAY 11

MAKE ALLOWANCES FOR EACH OTHER'S FAULTS

Therefore I, a prisoner for serving the Lord, beg you to lead a life worthy of your calling, for you have been called by God. Always be humble and gentle. Be patient with each other, making allowances for each other's faults because of you love.

EPHESIANS 4:1–2 NLT

Make allowance for each other's faults, and forgive anyone who offends you. Remember, the Lord forgave you, so you must forgive others. Above all, clothe yourselves with love, which binds us all together in perfect harmony.

COLOSSIANS 3:13–14 NLT

I think one of the hardest things to adjust to when we became a police family was all the change and unknown. Would my officer actually get home from work on time, or would he get stuck on a call? Would we be getting ready to go out the door to breakfast when he got the call for an overtime shift? Would we be in the middle of making holiday plans when a schedule changed and he had to work the days we were just planning on being gone?

In the midst of constant change and uncharted waters, there's an enormous need for grace. It's pretty easy to get angry when our officer is called in for overtime; I've definitely been there before. We can roll our eyes and huff and puff when the training schedule gets switched around and we have to change our Friday night plans, or when we need to move our weekend away around on the calendar—yet again. Those things used to frustrate me to no end, and usually I would end up taking out that frustration on my officer. But I soon learned that: 1) those things aren't my officer's fault, 2) there's not much we can do about it, and 3) we *can* choose how we react to it.

I've realized (through a lot of trial and error) that life is a lot smoother and more enjoyable when I choose to let some things go. Adjusting plans and changing dates may be a pain, but it isn't the end of the world. I've felt the irritation of the constant mess that this life is, but I know it's a lot more manageable when I choose to let some of those things go. Blue life is not easy. There's an immense need for flexibility, and there's a hefty need for forgiveness, patience, and love. Jesus was great at all these things, and when we look to Him for guidance, we can be too. What worries can you let go of today? What area can you choose to surrender to Him this week?

PRAYER

Lord, You have given us such an example of forgiveness and grace. When we fall short, when we sin, and when we stray, still

You are merciful. Please help us embody those traits in our lives and in our marriages. Remind us to love before we speak, judge, or act. Remind us to look to You, even when-and especially when-it's difficult..

DAY 12

GUARD YOUR HEART ABOVE ALL ELSE

Guard your heart above all else, for it determines the course of your life.
PROVERBS 4:23 NLT

Don't copy the behavior and customs of this world, but let God transform you into a new person by changing the way you think. Then you will learn to know God's will for you, which is good and pleasing and perfect.
ROMANS 12:2 NLT

Blessed are the pure in heart, for they will see God.
MATTHEW 5:8

There are a lot of painful, unhealthy, and damaging things in this world. And unfortunately, our officers face a lot of these things head on during every shift. As a police family, we're constantly surrounded by negativity, and this can take a toll on our hearts.

To combat all the negativity we see and feel, we must guard our hearts. We can do this by spending time in the Word—by making sure our actions are rooted in truth. We can do this by surrounding ourselves with people who build us up—those iron-sharpens-iron friends. And, most importantly, we can guard our hearts by staying in prayer.

Guarding our heart doesn't mean hiding from people. It doesn't mean hiding from love or hiding from life. It does, however, mean being mindful about what we expose ourselves to. Do we find that the more we watch violent TV shows or read suspenseful books, the higher our stress level is or the lower our patience? Or do we find that we sleep better when we watch a funny movie before bed or spend a little extra time reading Scripture?

Guarding our hearts also means being intentional to overcome what weighs us down. Did you have a particularly rough day? After you've pulled into the garage, spend an extra moment in the car after with your praise music on. Did your officer come home from a shift looking particularly defeated? Give him an extra smooch and say an extra prayer for him. We can't always control what negativity we face, but we can be careful about what we let seep into our life, home, and marriage. Be vigilant about guarding and protecting your heart, for everything else flows from it. How are you choosing to guard your heart today?

PRAYER

Lord, You have created us in Your image, and for that we are so grateful. Create in me a pure heart, and help me guard that heart from the things that work to weaken it. Remind me to stay in worship and prayer with You, God, especially on the days that the Enemy is relentless in his pursuit of my heart. Let me stay steadfast, and may my eyes be focused on You. Let my officer be not discouraged by the evil he faces but encouraged by You.

DAY 13

I WILL PERSONALLY GO WITH YOU AND GIVE YOU REST

And the Lord said, "I will personally go with you, Moses, and I will give you rest—everything will be fine for you."
EXODUS 33:14 NLT

Then Jesus said, "Come to me, all of you who are weary and carry heavy burdens, and I will give you rest."
MATTHEW 11:28 NLT

I don't know about you, but I find blue life exhausting. The shift work, constant stress and worry, and irregular schedules can really take a toll on us as families. As a police wife I know you're basically a superhero, but still, managing the house and family and schedule isn't easy.

When my officer first began this career, I took it upon myself to always be on top of things. Always cooking, cleaning, and picking up the slack—and often sacrificing my sleep and sanity in the process. I still love blessing my officer with a clean house and yummy dinner, but I'm now more cognizant of making sure that I take care of myself too.

Rest is referenced often throughout the Bible. In fact, we were specifically created to need rest. It isn't selfish or weak; it's what God intended for us. We are reminded time and time again to reach out to the Lord for rest, and when we do, it will be given to us. When we are weary, He is alert. When we are burdened, He is there to help us unload.

Today I urge you to take some time to get the rest you need. Maybe it's physical rest; your body really needs an extra thirty minutes of sleep. Or perhaps it is spiritual rest; you need some uninterrupted time with your Bible or a praise music playlist on repeat. It could even be mental rest; make a to-do list to unload all the thoughts swimming around in your busy brain, and curl up with a movie instead of the next project on your list.

Take some time to rest today. It's what we were created to do. Pick one small sliver of time or relaxing thing to do, and mark it down your schedule-and make it happen.

PRAYER

Lord, I reach out to you weary. Please help me get the rest I so desperately need. Place Your gentle arms around me and lull me to sleep. Quiet the thoughts in my head and slow the stress in my heart. Remind me that You have created me for rest and that taking care of myself is not selfish or silly, but a necessity.

DAY 14

RETURN TO ME WITH YOUR FULL HEART

"I will give them hearts that recognize me as the Lord. They will be my people, and I will be their God, for they will return to me wholeheartedly."
JEREMIAH 24:7 NLT

"Come, let us return to the LORD. He has torn us to pieces but he will heal us; he has injured us but he will bind up our wounds."
HOSEA 6:1

They replied, "Believe in the Lord Jesus and you will be saved, along with everyone in your household."
ACTS 16:31 NLT

If we're being honest, there have been times when I've strayed from God. Boy, have I strayed. Sometimes it's been because of a certain life event; a tragedy happened and I've questioned my faith or simply been angry with God. Other times I've allowed myself to be pulled away by something worldly and given my attention to something other than God. And sometimes I've simply gotten lazy with my faith; I've put off my reading, I've prayed less, or I've skipped church for weeks on end.

The Bible tells many stories of people who've strayed, and if we take a peek on Facebook or have a conversation with a coworker, we know plenty of people from our own lives who have strayed as well. We were made human and imperfect and with free will, and this means that at times we're going to stray from our God and our faith. The amazing thing is that when this happens, we can return to the Lord.

Our God is a God of grace and love and forgiveness. Each time we stray from Him, He welcomes us home with open arms. When we return to God with our whole heart, He is pleased.

Blue life gives us plenty of opportunities to stray. Things happen to our officers that make us question our faith and our God. Things get busy and we let our faith take the backseat. But regardless of our circumstances or how far we might roam, the Lord is waiting for us to return to Him—and waiting joyfully with open arms. Have you been feeling the pull to come back to Him with your full heart one day? Make that day today.

PRAYER

Lord, You are so gracious and forgiving. Each time I've strayed from You, You've welcomed me back with open arms. You're patient with my journey and remain the same, no matter how I struggle. Thank you for Your merciful heart and Your good plans.

DAY 15

BE SILENT AND GET RID OF BITTERNESS AND RAGE

"The LORD will fight for you; you need only to be still."
EXODUS 14:14

Get rid of all bitterness, rage and anger, brawling and slander, along with every form of malice. Be kind and compassionate to one another, forgiving each other, just as in Christ God forgave you.
EPHESIANS 4:31–32

The other day I was walking to dinner with my officer and a friend. We were laughing and chatting down the sidewalk, almost to our destination, when it happened. "&#%$ the police!" we heard from right up the street, and a grinning man waved one finger (you know the one) at us through his open car window before driving off, leaving me dusty and heartbroken.

Sigh. I know you've had the same experience, or at least a similar one. As blue families we're often targeted by those who express their hatred toward police—and therefore, our officers and ourselves.

Each and every time, I hate it. I hate the feeling it brings. I hate the fear it instills in me, even if for just a second. I hate the reminder it serves that my officer is in a dangerous profession. I hate that he deals with these people—these hateful, angry people—every single day.

But hate plus hate doesn't equal anything but ... hate, does it? As hard as it is to shake those words and experiences off, that's exactly what I try to do. As hard as it is to log into Instagram and delete the comments attacking our officers and our family, that's what I do. And as hard as it is to kiss my officer goodbye each day, not knowing if he'll be the next one targeted lethally, that's what I do.

And each time, I pray. I pray for strength, for forgiveness, for grace, for patience, and for protection. I've looked (oh, how I've I looked) and I can't find anywhere in the Bible where we're told to scream back at the haters on the street or type furious words in response to the keyboard cowards. But I can find a lot of examples of grace, silence, and prayer.

So as hard as that is, that's what I try to do. Is it easy? No. But is it what we're called to do? I think so. What's a tough area or a hard person that you're choosing to pray for today?

PRAYER

Lord, You know how hard this life can be for us. You see how I struggle to keep my mouth shut to those who sling hatred toward us. You know how I hurt when I hear words being flung toward us. I pray that You'll give me the grace and strength to navigate those situations in ways that bring You glory. I pray that You'll continue to keep Your arms of safety wrapped around my officer. And I pray for those who hate our officers, that You might soften their hearts and open their eyes to the sacrifices that are made for them each day.

DAY 16

SERVE ONE ANOTHER HUMBLY IN LOVE

You ... were called to be free. But do not use your freedom to indulge in the flesh; rather, serve one another humbly in love.

GALATIANS 5:13

"For even the Son of Man did not come to be served, but to serve, and to give his life as a ransom for many."

MARK 10:45

I despise sewing. I really do. It's never been something I've done much, so I just haven't practiced and therefore I'm really rotten at it. It takes me ages to thread the needle; I always fray the thread. I even have difficulties tying off the thread when I've finally finished whatever project I'm attempting. In short, the entire process is one I would much rather skip.

But the other week, a button came off my officer's duty shirt. After much searching I found an old academy shirt with similar buttons on it, buried deep in the closet. I clipped the button off the old shirt, and my officer used fabric glue to stick it to the proper spot on his uniform. But of course, a few days later he told me that it had come off halfway through his shift. So I cut off a new button, spent ten minutes trying to tie a knot in the thread, and sloppily sewed it back on (with some glue for added support, because let's be honest, it needed all of the help it could get).

I hate sewing, but I love my officer. One of our biggest callings in life is to serve others, and that includes serving our spouses and our families. Being the hands and feet of Jesus means using our hands and feet to carry out Jesus-like actions in our daily lives. In this case, that action was sewing on a pesky black button when I'd rather be catching up on laundry (okay, Netflix) and drinking more coffee. I am nowhere near perfect, but that's okay, because Jesus' love is. When we show that love to others, we're spreading His perfect love in our world.

And isn't that something we could always use more of? How are you using your hands and feet to serve out God's love today?

PRAYER

Lord, You have created us to serve so well. Every detail of our bodies, every part of our minds, was designed by You to help carry out Your perfect plan. Thank you for creating me to be competent and compassionate. Thank you for blessing me with my officer, who is perfectly made for me. I praise You for the opportunities You give me to serve him and others, because I know it brings You joy to see Your children being Your hands and feet.

DAY 17

THE THORNS THAT DISTRACT US

"This is the meaning of the parable: The seed is the word of God. Those along the path are the ones who hear, and then the devil comes and takes away the word from their hearts, so that they may not believe and be saved. Those on the rocky ground are the ones who receive the word with joy when they hear it, but they have no root. They believe for a while, but in the time of testing they fall away. The seed that fell among thorns stands for those who hear, but as they go on their way they are choked by life's worries, riches and pleasures, and they do not mature. But the seed on good soil stands for those with a noble and good heart, who hear the word, retain it, and by persevering produce a crop."

LUKE 8:11–15

The other day I was sitting in our living room, having my morning quiet time, when I heard ... voices? The audible murmur of conversation was coming from upstairs! I slowly crept up the stairs, poked my head tentatively into our office, and ... saw that my officer's radio was still on from his last shift.

Sigh. Crisis averted! I switched the radio off, made sure that it was charging, and went back down to my cozy spot on the couch. And then I got to thinking. In a world as busy as ours, it's extremely easy to get distracted. I looked around our living room and immediately spotted the TV, a tablet, my open laptop on the table, two phones (work and personal), and my full planner spilling over with appointments and to-do lists.

It made me think of the parable that Jesus told in Luke 8, of the seeds that are scattered and the obstacles that get in their way. The seed that was sown among the thorns didn't blossom because it was choked out by the worldly things in life, like worries, temptations, and distractions. We ourselves are constantly bombarded by those things. Some of them are clearly from Satan and some are not as blatant; they just show up as little distractions. Maybe it's our job, maybe it's our pursuit to keep up with the Joneses, or maybe it's simply the TV playing in the background (or a radio going off upstairs).

We will have different thorns in our life and they will always be there, trying to stifle our growth and drag us further away from God. We must work hard at being aware of what these thorns look like and be diligent at fighting them off, focusing on cultivating the life that Jesus has planned for us instead of falling into the trap that fear and sin is trying to entangle us in.

Blue life contains plenty of its own thorns, but when we

work hard at intentionally moving toward soil that is rich and plentiful, we will reap the harvest for ourselves, our officers, and our families.

PRAYER

Lord, You have sown me carefully and intentionally. Although this world is full of distractions and sins, I want to live a life that is fruitful. Help me be aware of the things that seek to separate me from You. Help me focus on You and Your Word and not on the distractions that insert their way into my life. Let my life and my home be one that has rich, plentiful soil—one that is rooted deeply in You and Your Word. Help my officer and me plant words of truth in our home and reap daily the things that You have planned for us.

DAY 18

IRON SHARPENS IRON

As iron sharpens iron, so a friend sharpens a friend.
PROVERBS 27:17 NLT

Whoever walks with the wise becomes wise, but the companion of fools will suffer harm.
PROVERBS 13:20 ESV

"There is no greater love than to lay down one's life for one's friends."
JOHN 15:13 NLT

The older I've gotten, the more I've realized how precious real friends are. The friends who are there for you in the good times and the bad. The friends who build you up and also keep you honest and humble. The ones who show up in the middle of the night when you need them and the ones who you can sit in silence with and still be comfortable.

When God created us, He didn't intend for us to be alone. Humans were created for relationship—with our spouse, with our family, and with our friends. This is especially important in this blue life that can be extremely isolating and lonely if we allow it.

I know there are days when you just want to curl up on the sofa and talk to no one. I know there are times when having someone over for dinner seems too daunting. I know there are evenings when you want to pass on your neighbor's invitation to come watch the game. And sometimes, that's fine. But I urge you to take those people—your people—up on their offers for community. Invest in your friendships. Pick up the phone. Go on walks with your girlfriends and go out for double dates with your couple friends. Join a small group or start a small Bible study.

It's said that we're the sum of the five people we keep closest to us. Who is in your circle? Are you keeping them close? Are they sharpening you?

PRAYER

Lord, I will never forget how much You have blessed me with friendship. We are loved by You as Your precious children, and we are loved by each other. You have given us such a gift in each friend that You send our way and place in our lives. I pray that You'll deepen these friendships, that You'll protect these friendships, and that You'll bless these friendships.

DAY 19

PERHAPS THIS IS THE MOMENT FOR WHICH YOU HAVE BEEN CREATED

"For if you keep silent at this time, relief and deliverance for the Jews will arise from another place, but you and your father's family will perish. And who knows but that you have come to your royal position for such a time as this?"

ESTHER 4:14

This is often translated "Perhaps this is the moment for which you were created."

"But I have raised you up for this very purpose, that I might show you my power and that my name might be proclaimed in all the earth."

EXODUS 9:16

And we know that God causes everything to work together for the good of those who love God and are called according to his purpose for them.

ROMANS 8:28 NLT

When my officer took his oath and officially became part of the blue family, it wasn't just he who dedicated his life to this career; it was both of us. Marriage calls us to serve side by side with our spouse, and when our officer has been called to serve a blue life, our role as their wife is especially important.

We are not "just a wife." We are not just "Officer So-and-So's spouse." When we married our officer, we made the decision to become one. This means we made the choice to help him carry his burdens, to support him, to love him, and to walk alongside him—through the good and the bad.

When I think of stepping into one's calling, I remember the story of Esther. I think of a poor orphaned girl who found favor with the Lord and saved her people. I know that's the most abridged summary ever, but really, who better emulates someone stepping into their role and calling than she? Some of us married our officers when they were already part of blue life, and some of us knew our officers way before they were "Officer." Some of us feel like we're crushing police wife life, and some of us constantly question whether we can handle this calling or not.

You can.

At my officer's Christmas party last year, his chief stood up to say a few words. He talked briefly about our officers and their sacrifices, but he spent a lot more time talking to the families who were there. Thanking us. Recognizing that our officers can't do this life alone.

Even when it feels like our lives revolve around the badge and the chaotic life it causes, our simple presence can make all the difference. We've all heard that God made the toughest women police wives, and I know this is true.

You have other callings in life, but your calling as police wife will always be important.

PRAYER

Lord, thank you for choosing me to be my officer's wife. Even though this life is hard and crazy, there's no other life I would rather live. I'm privileged that my officer chose me as his bride, and I'm honored that You chose us to walk this thin blue line together. Give us strength as we navigate the mountains and valleys of this life, and give us an abundance of grace for each other. Remind me of how important my role is as my officer's wife, especially when I feel like I'm not enough. Remind me that You have created me to be strong and courageous, kind and graceful, humble and patient, and, most important, a follower of You.

DAY 20

LOVE YOUR ENEMIES

"Love your enemies! Do good to them. Lend to them without expecting to be repaid. Then your reward from heaven will be very great, and you will be truly acting as children of the Most High, for he is kind to those who are unthankful and wicked."
Luke 6:35 NLT

"But I tell you, love your enemies and pray for those who persecute you."
Matthew 5:44

"I have told you all this so that you may have peace in me. Here on earth you will have many trials and sorrows. But take heart, because I have overcome the world."
John 16:33 NLT

I consider myself a pretty tolerant person. My degrees are in social work, so I've taken countless classes and workshops on ethics, equality, and advocating. The majority of my clients are not exactly pro-police; in fact, most are the opposite. One day I had a session with a family who lived in an apartment complex in the worst part of town, and when I came out into the parking lot afterward, I stopped frozen in my tracks.

I'd had a thin blue line sticker on my car for years. It was a small black one in the shape of our state with a tiny blue line running through it—small, barely noticeable, and tucked in the upper corner of my back windshield. But when I came out to the parking lot that day, it was torn off my car and ripped to pieces on the ground.

At first I was scared. I spotted it strewn on the asphalt and immediately glanced around at the people milling about the parking lot and hanging out the nearby windows, wondering if it was one of them. My hand went to the pepper spray in my bag and I quickly hurried into my car and locked the doors, reversing and leaving the property as soon as possible. A few minutes down the road, once I was in a section of town that felt safer, I pulled into a coffee shop parking lot, turned off my car (but kept the doors locked), and let my eyes start well up.

I still felt scared, but I was also mad. It enraged me that someone had the audacity to vandalize my personal car. I felt victimized simply because of my blue support. But mostly, I felt sad that this is the world we live in.

My heart hurt as I thought of the officers we've lost in the line of duty and specifically those targeted simply for being cops. Our officers put their lives on the line every day for our communities, whether they're thankful or not. We kiss them goodbye each day not knowing if they're going to walk back through our front door. We sacrifice holidays, weekends, dinners, and a nine-to-five.

And we should be proud of all that. We should be proud of our officers and their calling, and we should be proud of ourselves for supporting them. But there will always be those who disagree. There will always be people who rip down our blue-support stickers and flags, egg our patrol cars, stare down our thin blue line shirts, and say cruel words when they see us out with our uniformed husband.

Regardless of this, be proud. Keep loving your officer. Keep supporting him, and his brothers and sisters in blue, in whichever way you feel led. And keep praying for the people who hate our officers so much.

For we know who holds tomorrow, friends. We know whose hand is protecting us. Take heart in this world, for God's love is bigger than any of the giants we face. And that love and power is in you.

PRAYER

Lord, You know my heart. You know how discouraging it can be when the world lashes out at my officer and my family. Please take that discouragement and turn it into encouragement. Remind me of the goodness of our world and of Your Word. Help keep my officer and me encouraged when it seems like the world is ganging up on us, because You, almighty Lord, are on our side. Even though it's through gritted teeth, help me pray for those who wish evil upon our blue family. Soften their hearts, Lord, and let them see our officers for who they are—human.

DAY 21

LET MY WORDS REMAIN IN YOU

"Study this Book of Instruction continually. Meditate on it day and night so you will be sure to obey everything written in it. Only then will you prosper and succeed in all you do."
Joshua 1:8 NLT

Let the peace of Christ rule in your hearts, since as members of one body you were called to peace. And be thankful. Let the message of Christ dwell among you richly as you teach and admonish one another with all wisdom through psalms, hymns, and songs from the Spirit, singing to God with gratitude in your hearts.
Colossians 3:15–16

"If you remain in me and my words remain in you, ask whatever you wish, and it will be done for you."
John 15:7

Colossians is one of my favorite books in the Bible. I love the nuggets of wisdom hidden among its pages and the comfort I get when reading it through. One of my favorite chapters is Colossians 3, in which we're reminded to set our hearts and minds on things above, not on earthly things. That chapter really hits home for me, because I'll be the first to admit that my mind often gets clogged up with worldly things. I think about my to-do list, I worry about my officer while he's at work, I compose work emails in my mind, and sometimes I just have random bits of a podcast or book floating around in my head. What should be taking up a majority of that space is Scripture.

I think back to the time when my officer was in academy and had to memorize countless laws and speeches. We all know the beginning of the Miranda Warning (thanks, *Law & Order*!), but our officers have it memorized inside and out. When they present a driver with a speeding ticket, they recite "the spiel" without a second thought. When they book someone in jail, they rattle off their charges and rights by second nature.

What if, when situations presented themselves in our life, we were able to immediately deliver a Scripture to go with it? I love when I'm facing a battle or plotting a next step and a relevant and perfectly timed verse pops into my head. Many times when I'm marinating on a topic, I'll open up my Bible and page through it, looking for a passage that's applicable to what I'm thinking about. And often, throughout my week, I'll ask for a Scripture verse to be made known to me during prayer.

Reading our Bibles and memorizing Scripture is not always easy—at least not for me. It's something I have to work hard at and carve specific time out for. But each time

I'm thinking about something or having a discussion and a relevant verse spills out of my lips, I feel comforted and I feel faithful.

Let's work hard to fill out minds with God's promises and follow through by taking His advice. Let those words come out of our mouths as easily and assuredly as the Miranda Rights come out of our officer's during his shift.

PRAYER

Lord, thank you for giving us Your Word to marinate on. In times of distress and in times of joy, let Your words pop into my mind. Help me stay focused during my quiet times to read and memorize Scripture. Let those words spill out of my mouth throughout the day and dance around in my head at night.

DAY 22

NOTHING CAN SEPARATE US FROM GOD'S LOVE

For I am convinced that neither life nor death, neither angels nor demons, neither the present nor the future, nor any powers, neither height nor depth, nor anything else in all creation, will be able to separate us from the love of God that is in Christ Jesus our Lord.

ROMANS 8:38–39

"Though the mountains be shaken and the hills be removed, yet my unfailing love for you will not be shaken nor my covenant of peace be removed," says the LORD, who has compassion on you.

ISAIAH 54:10

"Never will I leave you, never will I forsake you."

HEBREWS 13:5

One of my favorite quotes comes from Corrie ten Boom: "There is no pit so deep, that God's love is not deeper still."[1] Each time I look at those profound words, they resonate in my gut. What a love! A love so deep and so full that we can't mess it up, no matter what we do. What a God! A God who loves us so fiercely and so completely that even in all our imperfect human ways we can't drift too far or fail too miserably. There is nothing—*nothing!*—that we can do or that this world can throw at us that can separate us from God when we look to Him.

Whew. What a love! In our broken world we are presented with many opportunities to screw up, to stray, or to sin. We work hard at earning and keeping things. If we stop showing up at work for a week, for example, we probably won't have a job to come back to. If we stop putting effort into our relationships, we probably won't have a friend for that much longer. If we self-sabotage an opportunity or a relationship, then we will most likely see it slip through our fingertips.

And yet that's not possible with God. God, who is bigger and more valuable than any job or friend or house or event, has told us that there's nothing we can do to earn His love, because we already have it.

You guys. What a promise! We must work to build our relationship with God, and we must dive into His Word and remember His Scriptures, but there's nothing that we can do—no way we can mess up—that will take God's love away from us when we reach out to Him. John 3:16 (arguably one of the most-known Scriptures worldwide) tells us that by believing, we have eternal life. What a precious gift.

PRAYER

Lord, I am so unworthy and so flawed, and yet You love me. Even when I feel like I've made mistakes and am undeserving, Your love still remains. You have promised that there's nothing on this earth that can separate You from us, and for that I am so thankful. Draw me near to you, Lord.

DAY 23

BODY CAM FOOTAGE

Turn from evil and do good; seek peace and pursue it.
PSALM 34:14

Follow my example, as I follow the example of Christ.
1 CORINTHIANS 11:1

Don't let anyone look down on you because you are young, but set an example for the believers in speech, in conduct, in love, in faith and in purity.
1 TIMOTHY 4:12

It seems like every time I log into social media, there's a snippet of an officer's dashcam or personal recorder posted, or perhaps footage from an iPhone recording that a citizen took. Some of it is positive, like an officer rocking a baby or shooting hoops with a lone teenager. Most of it is negative. Like it or not, our officers are constantly under surveillance. During each shift, their words and actions are recorded by both their departments and the community, and it could be made public at any moment.

If you were to wear a bodycam, would you be proud of what it recorded? There's that saying that "character is what we do when no one is watching." A lot of times we're unaware which eyes are surveilling us. If you're a parent, you know your children are constantly watching you, imitating what you do and copying the words you say (both the good and the bad). We're also on display at our workplace, whatever that may look like. Through interactions with our coworkers and our boss, actions are noticed and language is observed. There are also our neighbors, the checkout lady at the store, the mail carrier delivering our Amazon Prime packages, and the driver in the next car over while we're stuck in traffic.

If you were to watch a highlight (or "lowlight") reel of your past month, would you be proud of what it showed? Or would you hang your head in embarrassment? I know I'd be a combination of both. We're called to live humble and quiet lives, but also to set an example that Christ Himself would be proud of. Even though our lives aren't recorded in the way our officer's shifts are, they do set an example to those around us. Is it an example we're proud of?

PRAYER

Lord, I know You're always with me and always watching over me. I also know that others are watching me too. I pray that You're proud of the life I'm leading and the example I'm setting. Lead me to live a life that proclaims Your name, God. Help me to make choices that glorify You, and give me a heart that discerns the actions and choices that best serve You.

DAY 24

YOU ARE NOT ALONE

Even though I walk through the darkest valley, I will fear no evil, for you are with me; your rod and your staff, they comfort me.

PSALM 23:4

Where can I go from your Spirit? Where can I flee from your presence? If I go up to the heavens, you are there; if I make my bed in the depths, you are there. If I rise on the wings of the dawn, if I settle on the far side of the sea, even there your hand will guide me, your right hand will hold me fast.

PSALM 139:7–10

"Therefore go and make disciples of all nations, baptizing them in the name of the Father and of the Son and of the Holy Spirit, and teaching them to obey everything I have commanded you. And surely I am with you always, to the very end of the age."

MATTHEW 28:19–20

How often do we feel like we're the "only one" going through something? How often do we feel like it's just us who is stumbling? The Enemy loves to make us feel alone and detached. In fact, that's often when he preys on us the most. He gets us to alienate ourselves and put a wedge between ourselves and God, tricking us into thinking that we're crazy or unlovable or broken.

Friends, that's a lie.

Blue life can be very isolating. It feels strange to celebrate Easter on a Tuesday and kiss our officers goodbye for work at eight p.m. It can feel shameful to tell our boss that no, we don't need a plus one to the holiday party, and embarrassing to tell our friends that yes, he'll be missing yet another dinner. It's easy to think that we're the only one who doesn't have that picture-perfect family with the white picket fence. That we're companionless. Abandoned. Detached.

That's a lie too.

In Psalm 139 David says that no matter where he goes, the Lord is there. He couldn't escape him, and neither can we. Wherever we go, wherever we flee, wherever we hide—His love is there. When we cry out to God, He is there. He doesn't miss dinners or holidays, and He doesn't care if we do our devotionals at five p.m. or five a.m. We're never alone, because God is always with us. Even in a life that can be isolating and trying, He is here, and we are never alone.

PRAYER

Lord, You are constant and You are present. Thank you for

always being here. When I feel lonely, let You presence be known. When the Enemy's lies try to tell me that I'm alone, remind me of Your truths. Let Your comfort be enough for me, God, and wrap my family in Your arms.

DAY 25

WHILE I WAIT, YOU STRENGTHEN MY HEART

Wait for the LORD; be strong and take heart and wait for the LORD.

PSALM 27:14

So Jacob served seven years to get Rachel, but they seemed like only a few days to him because of his love for her.

GENESIS 29:20

But the Holy Spirit produces this kind of fruit in our lives: love, joy, peace, patience, kindness, goodness, faithfulness, gentleness, and self-control. There is no law against these things!

GALATIANS 5:22–23 NLT

Police wife life seems to consist primarily of waiting. It's waiting for that next text or call back, that vacation request to go through, that shift to end, that uniform to dry, and mostly for that front door to open and our officer to come walking through it, safe and sound. I don't know about you, but I've never been very good at waiting. Patience isn't something that comes naturally to me, but is a skill I need to work diligently at improving.

Being patient and waiting gracefully goes against most things our culture stands for. We live in a world that is rapidly paced, and a lot of times we're told to "get after it" and "get ahead"; stepping on people or cutting corners to do so is often acceptable. That might be what our world says, but so many stories in the Bible tell us the opposite. We're taught over and over to wait—expectantly and eagerly—but wait all the same.

It's not surprising, then, that patience is a fruit of the Spirit. It's something that God looks fondly upon. If we summed up the entirety of the Bible in a few simple sentences, one of those sentences would contain something about waiting for Jesus to return. As Christians and as police wives, patience is something that isn't just encouraged but is a necessity.

When I think of waiting for a loved one, I think of Jacob waiting for Rachel. He spent years working to earn her hand in marriage, but we read that those years felt "like only a few days" because he loved her so intensely. What a precious thought! As we wait for our officers to return home, let that waiting shape our hearts. Let that waiting increase the love we have for our officers, and in turn strengthen our marriages and our faith. Let patience be something that is valued in our homes, and something that brings us closer to our officer and to God.

PRAYER

Lord, today I ask You to help me build my patience. Let me wait eagerly and not impatiently. Let me remain expectant, no matter how long I have to wait. Help shape my heart into one that waits gracefully and my spirit into one that overflows with patience, because that is what You want for me.

DAY 26

GOD'S COMFORT IS ENOUGH

"Is God's comfort too little for you? Is his gentle word not enough?"
JOB 15:11 NLT

Cast your cares on the LORD and he will sustain you; he will never let the righteous be shaken.
PSALM 55:22

Come near to God and he will come near to you.
JAMES 4:8 NLT

One of my favorite comfort foods is a big bowl of mac and cheese. There's something about the mixture of warm carbs and cheesiness combined with the reminder of carefree childhood days that automatically puts me at ease. It's not a fix-all, of course—it's just food—but on the days when I want nothing more than to crawl into bed, it offers a bit of comfort. A cozy, carby, cheesy embrace in a bowl.

We look for a lot of things to provide us comfort in this life. Just like mac and cheese, I also turn to a hot mug of coffee, a warm toasty fire, and my officer's sturdy arms in the hard times when I need a little extra pick-me-up. All these comforting things help ease my anxiety, calm my fears, and perk me back up after a rough day.

You know what else does this, perfectly and without fail? Jesus.

I think sometimes we unintentionally underestimate God's comforting hand in our life. Maybe we get swept up in the material things in life or our daily drama. Maybe we think our problems are too small or silly to bring to Him. Maybe we don't always feel God's comfort in the ways we think we need to. Whatever it is, I sometimes find myself running to the wrong sources of comfort and coming away still feeling hollow.

We're told over and over that when we reach out to God, He reaches down to us. When we tell Him our struggles, He listens. He will sustain us and comfort us, and in this crazy blue life, we need a lot of that. Cast your cares on Him, because He cares for you.

PRAYER

Lord, draw near to me. Let Your presence be known. Wrap Your arms around me and my family. Let the winds whisper Your name and my heart be settled in Your peace. You know I have struggles, but I know You're bigger than any of my problems and mightier than any demons I may face. Comfort me and my officer, Lord. We trust You to hold us.

DAY 27

LIVING BOLDLY

After this prayer, the meeting place shook, and they were all filled with the Holy Spirit. Then they preached the word of God with boldness.

ACTS 4:31 NLT

So we say with confidence, "The Lord is my helper; I will not be afraid. What can mere mortals do to me?"

HEBREWS 13:6

I also pray that you will understand the incredible greatness of God's power for us who believe him. This is the same mighty power that raised Christ from the dead and seated him in the place of honor at God's right hand in the heavenly realms.

EPHESIANS 1:19 NLT

The first time I rode along with my officer, I was struck by how bold he was during his shift. Keep in mind that I've known him for almost my entire life and have spent the better part of a decade as his significant other. But seeing him at work, in his role of "Officer," was completely different from anything else I had experienced with him in all of our time together.

Whether he was running code to a suspected DV or knocking on the door of a potentially hostile home, he was calm and confident. As I sat in the passenger seat of his patrol car, watching him work, my heartbeat quickened in my chest. What if one of these calls turned into one of *those* calls—one that ended badly? What if something happened to him? What if ...

And as I sat there, watching in awe as my officer conducted his calls professionally and courageously, I thought of what a perfect example he showed of boldly walking in his calling. Being a police officer, especially in this hostile climate, is not an easy job. Arriving to dangerous calls involving complete strangers who may or may not appreciate your presence isn't easy. It would be easier to let someone else do it. It would be easier to shrink back and hide.

But that's not what our officers do, and that's not who God created us to be. We were created to be bold, righteous, powerful, and faithful. We were intricately stitched together to pray prayers that move mountains and cure diseases, that change lives and proudly proclaim the gospel. Just as our officers boldly perform their duties each shift, we are to boldly live our lives as a testament to the goodness and power the Lord has bestowed onto each of us.

PRAYER

Lord, thank you for creating my officer. Let him be an example of boldly living out his calling and his faith. Open my eyes to see this, Lord, and remind me to pray bold, powerful prayers. Remind me to live out my faith courageously and confidently. Remind me that You did not create us to live small lives or pray small prayers. You created us in Your image, God, and have given us the power to touch lives and spread Your Word. Let us live lives that are powerful testaments of Your goodness.

DAY 28

AND IF NOT, HE IS STILL GOOD

"But even if he does not, we want you to know, Your Majesty, that we will not serve your gods or worship the image of gold you have set up."
Daniel 3:18
It is often translated to "And if not, he is still good."

And we know that in all things God works for the good of those who love him, who have been called according to his purpose.
Romans 8:28

Furthermore, because we are united with Christ, we have received an inheritance from God, for he chose us in advance, and he makes everything work out according to his plan.
Ephesians 1:11 NLT

For a while now, I've picked a "verse of the year" each January. It's a verse that resonates with me and the season I'm going through and is something to hold on to throughout the coming year. Some years these verses immediately pop into my mind, and sometimes I need to pray about them for what seems like ages. A few years ago was a big year of transition for my officer and me. We had just graduated college, moved across the country, and I had begun grad school in a brand-new town. This was also the time when my officer began applying for jobs in his chosen field—law enforcement. This aligned with his degree and had been our plan for the past several years.

Opportunities came and went. He had interviews. He turned in applications. He spent time on the phone with prospective agencies. We prayed and prayed and prayed. And after a seemingly perfect job slipped through our fingers and I was complaining to God about it, I felt Him ask, "Do you question my goodness because that specific opportunity didn't pan out?"

Oof. I was so convicted. And so my verse for that year became Daniel 3:18: "And if not, He is still good" (paraphrase). Even if that job doesn't work out, He is still good. Even if our living situations drastically change, He is still good. Even if it seems like everything is falling apart, He is still good.

Of course, things worked out in the end—according to His plan, not ours. And our faith became stronger as we learned to trust in that plan more and lean into God's comfort in our times of frustration and disappointment. Often when things don't go according to our agenda, or when bad things happen, we question God. We may begin to question our faith. But light still shines, even in—and especially in—the darkness. The darkness doesn't extinguish the light, just as the evil in our world doesn't snuff out God's goodness. God's plan is still good, even when it differs greatly from our own.

Whether it's a promotion or a department change or a desire for a different shift, I challenge you to shift from a mindset of "my plan" to "His plan." And when things don't go as you hope, I pray that you'll remember that it doesn't affect His goodness.

For He is always, *always* good.

PRAYER

Lord, thank you for having a plan for me that is so much better than the one I drew up for myself. Thank you for being patient with me as I struggle to trust You completely. Thank you for the trials You put in front of my officer and I, as they have brought us closer to each other and to You. Lord, let us always remember Your goodness and Your good plans. Never let me forget that living in accordance to Your will is always the best route, even when other paths seem more tempting.

DAY 29

A FIRM FOUNDATION WILL NOT CRUMBLE

"Though the rain comes in torrents and the floodwaters rise and the winds beat against that house, it won't collapse because it is built on bedrock. But anyone who hears my teaching and doesn't obey it is foolish, like a person who builds a house on sand. When the rains and floods come and the winds beat against that house, it will collapse with a mighty crash."
Matthew 7:25–27 NLT

For no one can lay a foundation other than the one which is laid, which is Jesus Christ.
1 Corinthians 3:11

The wicked die and disappear, but the family of the godly stands firm.
Proverbs 12:7 NLT

If you ask a handful of police officers what the foundation of their training is, I would bet that most of them would say the academy. It was there that they learned the basics of policing, obtained training from experienced officers, memorized laws, and practiced hundreds of possible scenarios. Our officers will always have this training to fall back on throughout their careers. Yes, they still get ongoing training and are constantly honing their skills, but a lot of their policing instinct (their "muscle memory," if you will) is from the academy. Rightfully so, as it is meant to be the foundation for their careers.

Depending on your job, you might also have training or education that you consider the foundation of your work. We also have a foundation for our marriage, our family, and our life—and in our home, we choose the foundation of Jesus Christ.

Life is really good at throwing curve balls at us. Blue life is even better at it. As police families, our marriages are put under extra strain due to the stressful nature of our officers' jobs, the crazy hours, the missed holidays, and the intense and unique mindset that being an officer requires. Sometimes it can feel like we're a suspect in our own home. Sometimes it can feel like we go days without really seeing each other. Sometimes it can seem like this life is handing us way more than we can carry.

But even when we stumble, we have a firm foundation to lean on when Jesus is the rock on which our life is built. Just as our officers fall back on the skills they learned in academy, we fall back on whatever we have made a priority in our life. If that priority is our faith, we may slip and stumble, but we will not fall.

PRAYER

Lord, You have always been and always will be the foundation of our life. Let our marriage be built upon the strongest of all foundations—You. Let our family flourish because of its unbreakable foundation—You. Let our lives reflect Your steadfastness and everlasting faithfulness. When the tidal waves of life come rushing toward us, let us stand firm, as we know You are holding us steady.

DAY 30

KINDNESS

Be kind and compassionate to one another, forgiving each other, just as in Christ God forgave you.
EPHESIANS 4:32

But the Holy Spirit produces this kind of fruit in our lives: love, joy, peace, patience, kindness, goodness, faithfulness.
GALATIANS 5:22 NLT

Let love and faithfulness never leave you; bind them around your neck, write them on the tablet of your heart.
PROVERBS 3:3

The media loves to portray our officers as evil, racist, power-hungry monsters cowering behind their badges. As blue family we know that couldn't be further from the truth. Our officers display kindness in their jobs every day; it's just not considered newsworthy, and so the general public doesn't hear about it.

They don't hear about the single teenage mom our officer let off on a warning for having lapsed insurance because she's waiting for her paycheck to clear tomorrow. They don't hear about the elderly man our officer sat with for forty-five minutes while listening to him retell old war stories because he's lonely and doesn't have any grandchildren around. They don't hear about the tiny baby girl our officer rocked and cooed at for hours while waiting for child protective services to come and take her into custody.

We, as police wives, get to hear about some of these things some evenings (or mornings) when our officer makes it home from work. Sometimes we don't hear about them at all, as our officers are too exhausted or discouraged to remember to share those bright little snapshots with us. Because of all of this negativity, it can be even harder for our officers to remember the good that's in our world. It can be hard for us too, in a culture that no longer seems to prioritize kindness and good deeds. It's discouraging to only see negativity and backlash on the news, especially concerning our officers.

Fight back against that discouragement, friends. Fight back against the notion that only evil exists in our world. Good deeds are still noticed. Kindness is still valued. Be the neighbor who brings the newcomer a plate of cookies, be the friend who checks in regularly even when life is busy, and be the police wife who never stops praying. Be the one who encourages kindness, even if it goes unnoticed by the world, because it is always noticed by the One who values it the most.

PRAYER

Lord, You have created us to be kind, because we are created in Your image. You displayed the ultimate act of kindness when You sent Your Son to die for us. May we always remember the fruits of the Spirit and live them out each day, in our home and at our workplace. May the world's perception of our officers shift to see them for the kind and selfless souls that they are. And even if not, let us notice those acts each day and prioritize them in our families.

DAY 31

SPIRITUAL WARFARE

I also pray that you will understand the incredible greatness of God's power for us who believe him. This is the same mighty power that raised Christ from the dead and seated him in the place of honor at God's right hand in the heavenly realms.

EPHESIANS 1:19–20 NLT

And no wonder, for even Satan disguises himself as an angel of light.

2 CORINTHIANS 11:14

Put on the whole armor of God, that you may be able to stand against the devil's schemes.

EPHESIANS 6:11

I was in college before I really heard anyone talk about spiritual warfare, and it wasn't until I was almost twenty that I heard a pastor speak openly about the ways the Enemy tries to insert himself into our lives. Maybe it's because it's frightening and discouraging and icky, but it seems like we often shy away from discussing spiritual warfare. It's always going on around us, and there are countless ways that the Enemy deliberately tries to wedge himself between us and God. I might have learned about the concept of spiritual warfare years ago, but it wasn't until becoming a police wife that I saw it being acted out so forcefully each day.

Our officers are bombarded with the most hateful parts of our world each time they pull out of our driveways in their patrol cars. The people they interact with are often filled with hate, and their actions are usually far from Christlike. This makes it even more important to protect ourselves with the most powerful armor available—the armor of God.

There is nothing and no one stronger than God. No battle can be lost when we align our will with His. The devil flees when we arm ourselves with God's Word. Even though strong forces are working against our blue families, those evils will not prevail when we stay the course.

The mountains may crumble around us, but God's love will not. Our feet may stumble as we navigate these treacherous times, but our faith will remain strong. Evil may be all around us and the Enemy may be pounding on our doors, but the Lord's peace and protection will surround us. Take heart in the truth and not the warfare surrounding us. We may live in a broken world, but we serve a mighty and good God.

PRAYER

Lord, we live in a broken world, but we serve someone so much more powerful than all of the evil and the hate—You. Thank you for remaining faithful and strong. Thank you for being a force to be reckoned with. Let us cling to You, God, when the Enemy is pressing in. Let us surround ourselves with Your love instead of the evil that is floating around, vying for our marriages and our families. Help us to remain strong and faithful, and let us abide in Your love and protection.

DAY 32

WE WALK BY FAITH, NOT SIGHT

For we live by faith, not by sight.
2 CORINTHIANS 5:7

Now faith is confidence in what we hope for and assurance about what we do not see.
HEBREWS 11:1

So we fix our eyes not on what is seen, but on what is unseen, since what is seen is temporary, but what is unseen is eternal.
2 CORINTHIANS 4:18

Sometimes the sight of a patrol car parked in front of our house still surprises me. I drive around the corner into our neighborhood, my mind on work or what I'm about to make for dinner, and my heart leaps in my chest as my eyes spot the car. *Oh crap!* I think. *The cops are here!* I'm forgetting, of course, that I live with a cop.

There's frequently a patrol car in our driveway—and there has been for as long as we've lived in this house. But sometimes things aren't as they appear at first glance.

How many times has this happened to you? Maybe you hear a mumbled sentence from someone and react before fully understanding what they meant. Or maybe you, like me, had to do a double-take at something your eyes didn't quite focus on. This happens often in our life. We question the road before us, especially when we can only see the first little pathway.

In the Bible we read again and again that it's our faith that closes the gaps of knowledge and sight. Often we aren't sure of the road before us, but we are sure of our faith and God's goodness. Blue life holds many mysteries and unsure days. Each time our officer walks out the front door, we don't know when or if they'll walk back through it—but still, we have faith. Each call our officer goes on is unclear, but still they have faith. Let's let go of the need to see what is in front of us and instead cling to the promises of what's to come.

PRAYER

Lord, You have always remained faithful to me. Help me remember this in times when I'm having trouble taking a leap of faith. Let me always turn to You and Your Word, and let that guide my decisions. Help me to live out 2 Corinthians 5:7. Even when I can't see Your plan for my family, let me trust it, for Your plans are always good.

DAY 33

SABBATH

Then Jesus said to them, "The Sabbath was made to meet the needs of people, and not people to meet the requirements of the Sabbath."
MARK 2:27 NLT

By the seventh day God had finished the work he had been doing; so on the seventh day he rested from all his work. Then God blessed the seventh day and made it holy, because on it he rested from all the work of creating that he had done.
GENESIS 2:2–3

There remains, then, a Sabbath-rest for the people of God; for anyone who enters God's rest also rests from their works, just as God did from his.
HEBREWS 4:9–10

Ever since blue life began, our family's Sabbath has looked a little different than it did before my officer was "Officer." It no longer consists of traditional Sundays spent resting and going to church. We both work a lot of weekends, and we rarely make it to a traditional service on the traditional day and time. Sometimes we have our Sabbath days on a Saturday or a Tuesday, and sometimes it's just an afternoon or a morning. At first I felt guilty about this. After all, weren't we created to rest on Sundays? Isn't that the holy day?

But the more I prayed about it, the more I felt in my heart that it's not the day that matters; it's the intent. I'm confident that God doesn't hold it against our family that my officer is out serving and protecting on some Sundays, because in doing so he's answering his call. We also make the point to still schedule time to worship and rest as we used to do on Sunday, the traditional Sabbath day. In the book of Mark, we're told that Sabbath was created for us as a blessing, not a burden.

Others may feel differently, but our blue family makes our Sabbath whatever day we can. Whatever that day is, it always involved coffee, worship music, prayer, laughter, and rest. Usually it also involves a long walk, snuggles, and too many pancakes. Whenever our "Sundays" are, they're the days that rejuvenate my soul—just as Sabbath was created to do.

PRAYER

Lord, thank you for meeting me where I'm at. You know the chaos that blue life is, and You want rest for my officer and me. Let us cherish our Sabbath days. Let those days give our family rest and deepen our faith and gratitude for you, Lord. Help us protect our Sabbath days and prioritize them in our life, no matter how busy we might be. Let Your presence be known during these days, Lord, and let us rest in Your embrace.

DAY 34

BUILDING A BULLETPROOF LOVE

Love is patient, love is kind. It does not envy, it does not boast, it is not proud. It does not dishonor others, it is not self-seeking, it is not easily angered, it keeps no record of wrongs. Love does not delight in evil but rejoices with the truth. It always protects, always trusts, always hopes, always perseveres.

1 CORINTHIANS 13:4–7

Be completely humble and gentle; be patient, bearing with one another in love. Make every effort to keep the unity of the Spirit through the bond of peace.

EPHESIANS 4:2–3

My officer and I were together about eight years before he became "Officer," and before that we were friends. We grew up together and went through school together, and in doing so we learned about each other's quirks and strengths and how to pick each other up when the other was down. Our love has always been strong, but it's become a different kind of strong since he became an officer and we began this crazy blue life.

Blue life has taught us to be more patient with each other. Through the long shifts and ever-changing schedules and through the missed dinners and altered plans, we've had plenty of practice building our patience. We've learned to cherish our time together more and not take a slow evening or a Christmas morning together for granted. Through the swing shifts and changing schedules and missed holidays, we've learned that every moment we get together is a gift.

We've been reminded that each goodbye and out-the-door smooch could be the last, and to never part angry or bitter. We've realized that communication is not just good but a vital part of our relationship, and that the more we communicate the happier we are. We've learned that we don't have to do something fun to have fun together; some of our best memories are catching up over a home-cooked meal at the kitchen island or staying up late giggling in bed. We've made it a point to remember that a job is just a job, and family comes first. We've learned that teamwork does make the dream work and that we don't want to do this life with anyone else. We've learned and appreciated how vital our roles in one another's lives are. We've struggled and stumbled but we have *loved*.

Today I encourage you to think about the ways blue life has strengthened and blessed your relationship, instead of the ways it makes it difficult. Yes, blue life throws many curve balls at us and challenges our marriages in ways that other jobs don't, but it also gifts us with so many opportunities to strengthen our marriage and show our love. Since this blue life has begun, we've leaned on each other and on God more than ever. Think about those things today and share them with your officer, marinating on the goodness this life has brought to your family instead of the trials.

PRAYER

Lord, You are so good at teaching us lessons in the kindest of ways. Even through the mountains and valleys of this challenging career, You have made sure that we realize the gifts and blessings it is full of. Let us never forget about these blessings, God. In times of frustration and of heartbreak, remind us of the gift that this career is, the gift that our marriage is, and the beautiful gift our fellowship with You.

DAY 35

WHAT THE FUTURE HOLDS

"For I know the plans I have for you," declares the LORD, "plans to prosper you and not to harm you, plans to give you hope and a future."
JEREMIAH 29:11

But we are citizens of heaven, where the Lord Jesus Christ lives. And we are eagerly waiting for him to return as our Savior.
Philippians 3:20 NLT

"But seek first his kingdom and his righteousness, and all these things will be given to you as well. Therefore do not worry about tomorrow, for tomorrow will worry about itself. Each day has enough trouble of its own."
MATTHEW 6:33–34

Many days, right around the time that my officer should be coming home, I pull up our driveway cams to see if his patrol car is idling in front of the garage yet. I get eager to see him when I know it's time for him to be home, and check those cameras as I cook dinner or get ready for work, waiting for that telltale sign he's home.

Sometimes I wish I could pull up a "future cam" just as easily and see what life has in store for us. As someone who likes to know all the details and plan ahead, I occasionally feel anxious about the mysteries that lay ahead of us.

Throughout the Bible we're reminded that God knows the plan for our life. One of my favorite verses is Jeremiah 29:11. There's something so comforting about knowing with absolute certainty that the creator of this earth has also created a perfect plan for us. That's not to say that we'll never worry or have questions. Blue life can cause a lot of uncertainty. What will their shift be like? Will they make it home on time? Will they make it home at all? There are many what-ifs in law enforcement, but there are no what-ifs when it comes to our God.

Even though I still wish for a "future cam" every now and again, I know that whatever the future holds, it is good because He is good. When I feel myself begin to slip down the rabbit hole of worry, it's a good reminder to return to the cross. Instead of worrying, pray. Instead of wondering, ask. Instead of guessing, read. We may not know all the answers, but we know the One who does.

PRAYER

Lord, You have numbered every hair on my head and named every star in the sky. You have authored my story, and it is full of goodness. Thank you for intricately creating me and my story. Although I have questions and concerns about what the future holds for my officer and me, I know there's nothing to worry about because You hold the world. Help me rely on you, Lord, when I question the future. Help our family come to You for answers and trust what You say.

DAY 36

DID GOD REALLY SAY THAT?

Now the serpent was more crafty than any of the wild animals the LORD God had made. He said to the woman, "Did God really say, 'You must not eat from any tree in the garden'?"

GENESIS 3:1

Your word is a lamp for my feet, a light on my path.

PSALM 119:105

"Call to me and I will answer you and tell you great and unsearchable things you do not know."

JEREMIAH 33:3

I'm always impressed by my officer's ability to translate and understand everything that comes through his radio. Between the ten codes and the garbled speech, it's almost like a different language is coming out of that little speaker. During ride-alongs or when my officer is taking his lunch break at our kitchen island, I often find myself asking, "What was that?" or "Wait, did someone just say ___?"

Usually I'm wrong. Usually what I think I heard isn't correct, or it's only part of the story that's being transmitted. This makes me think back to the story of Genesis, and the way Satan twists our words and the Word of God. Centuries ago in the garden of Eden, through some crafty questioning and sly wording, Satan led Eve to believe that God was restricting her and Adam from eating any of the fruit. He made her believe that they were missing out because God just didn't want them to be happy. In reality, God asked them not to eat from one certain tree (not all of them) simply because He knew what was best for them.

The Enemy wants us to see God's Word as restrictive instead of freeing. He wants us to see God as rigid and distant instead of warm and loving. Just as our officer's radio can garble important words, the Enemy and the world jumble God's Word if we're not listening carefully. When what you're hearing or thinking comes out of fear, that's a good clue that it's not from God; it's from the Enemy. When you begin to question God and what He's telling you, go back to the Bible. Go back to your devotions and morning quiet time, and make sure you're filling your head and your heart with His Word and with prayer, instead of with the lies of this world.

PRAYER

Lord, You are kind and You are just. You want what's best for us, Your children, and do not operate as a strict dictator but as a loving father. Help me have ears to discern Your Word and eyes to see Your promises. Let me remain strong against the Enemy and the lies he tries to feed me and my family. Be present in my quiet times, Lord, and let me practice what it's like to hear Your voice so I can always pick it out of the garble that's transmitted every day in our busy and broken world.

DAY 37

GOD IS NOT ALWAYS FAIR, BUT HE IS ALWAYS JUST

He is the Rock, his works are perfect, and all his ways are just. A faithful God who does no wrong, upright and just is he.

DEUTERONOMY 32:4

If we claim to be without sin, we deceive ourselves and the truth is not in us. If we confess our sins, he is faithful and just and will forgive us our sins and purify us from all unrighteousness.

1 JOHN 1:8–9

One thing I learned right off the bat in our journey through blue life is that it's not fair. There are constant changes that are out of our control, like schedules and shifts and getting called in for overtime. Worse yet, we heartbreakingly lose officers to criminals and accidents—and that just doesn't make sense to our hurting hearts. Each time an officer is killed, we're reminded that life is so unfair. And it brings us to question, "Is God fair?"

He's not. He's not fair, but He is *always* just. Throughout the Bible we're reminded that this is true. God is impartial and judges "right" and "wrong" so much better than we try to. Therefore we're told that He is the only one who can judge us and will administer His justice accordingly. We see a lot of unfair things here on this earth and in this blue life. But all of that injustice is due to humans, not because of God. We were blessed with free will, and sometimes that free will is exercised for evil instead of good.

Because of our free will and our imperfection, we also often fall short. But God has told us that when we repent to Him, we are forgiven—no strings attached. When we come to God and ask for His hand in our lives because we have strayed, He forgives us. When we admit our shortcomings, He is there. Blue life is not fair, and we face a lot of trials, but our God is always faithful and He is always just.

PRAYER

Lord, thank you for being a just God. Thank you for being the One who judges us and administers justice in our lives. Although I don't always understand Your plan, I know that it's for good. Let me lean on You as the rock You are, and provide comfort and strength to our family when things happen that we don't understand. Put Your hand of protection around our blue family everywhere, and help us find solace in the fact that You have already written our stories and they are for good.

DAY 38

YOU ARE MORE

I praise you because I am fearfully and wonderfully made; your works are wonderful, I know that full well.
PSALM 139:14

Don't be concerned about the outward beauty of fancy hairstyles, expensive jewelry, or beautiful clothes. You should clothe yourselves instead with the beauty that comes from within, the unfading beauty of a gentle and quiet spirit, which is so precious to God.
1 PETER 3:3–4 NLT

She is more precious than rubies; nothing you desire can compare with her. Long life is in her right hand; in her left hand are riches and honor. Her ways are pleasant ways, and all her paths are peace. She is a tree of life to those who take hold of her; those who hold her fast will be blessed.
PROVERBS 3:15–18

She is clothed with strength and dignity; she can laugh at the days to come. She speaks with wisdom, and faithful instruction is on her tongue. She watches over the affairs of her household and does not eat the bread of idleness. Her children arise and call her blessed; her husband also, and he praises her.

PROVERBS 31:25–28

You are an incredible police wife. You do so much for your officer, and he couldn't get through life without you. But I also know that you're much more than just a LEOW. Maybe you're a mom or an auntie. A sister, a friend, a daughter, a professional, a maker, or a creator. Whatever else your titles may be, I know you have countless roles in life. Sometimes we get so swept up in blue life and our responsibilities there that we forget that we're also our own person. Being a police wife is one of my identities, and one that I am proud of, but I'm also many other things—a writer, a therapist, a traveler, an avid coffee drinker, and a loud laugher.

God has stitched each one us together purposefully and intricately. Our worth can be found throughout the pages of His love letters to us, and if we could see ourselves through His eyes, we would be nothing short of beautiful and flawless. This is contrary to our world and the culture that tells us to fixate on the things that need fixing. Do we need to lose a few pounds? Buy more expensive makeup? Put a better filter on that photo? No. What we really need to do is see ourselves through His eyes and marinate on how precious we are to Him. In a world that tells us to look at outward appearances, let us seek to look inward instead.

Today I encourage you not to undervalue your worth. Don't sell yourself short. You're not "just" a police wife. You are not "just" another woman, another worker, another mom, another neighbor. You are fearfully and wonderfully made. You are more precious than rubies. You are clothed in strength and dignity. You are the daughter of the Most High. You are chosen. You are redeemed. You are set apart.

PRAYER

Lord, I'm so grateful to be placed in the important role as my officer's spouse. Let me continue to support him and lift him up. Let me also remember that You have created me to be more than that. Remind me of all of my important roles, and of the person You have created me to be. I am the daughter of You, the King. You have set me apart. In times that I feel "just" or "less than," remind me of my worth. I am invaluable and I am worthy, because You are.

DAY 39

FOR GOD SO LOVED THAT HE GAVE

For God so loved the world that he gave his one and only Son, that whoever believes in him shall not perish but have eternal life.

JOHN 3:16

But God demonstrates his own love for us in this: While we were still sinners, Christ died for us.

ROMANS 5:8

But because of his great love for us, God, who is rich in mercy, made us alive with Christ even when we were dead in transgressions—it is by grace you have been saved.

EPHESIANS 2:4–5

There's a little church I pass on my way to work each morning that has a reader board out front. I've been driving that same route for over a year and I've never once seen it change. It has just one simple sentence on it: "For God so loved the world that He gave." It doesn't have the Scripture attribution next to it or the rest of the verse, but honestly, I like it better that way.

Sometimes when we look at that verse or even the Bible in its entirety, we forget the complexity of what God sacrificed for us. He gave His Son so we could have eternal life, yes—but can we take a step back and marinate on what that actually means? God loved this world—this broken, sinful world—so much that He gave. He gave His Son for us hopeless souls, so that we might have hope again. He gave us a second chance, and continues to give us chances each day. He gave us forgiveness that was so undeserved.

When I think of the magnitude of this, everything else seems to shrink. That disappointment I feel when discovering my officer has to work late doesn't seem as big of a deal. The impatience I feel when pulling into the coffee shop parking lot and seeing the long line decreases. The discouragement I feel when looking at my seemingly endless to-do list lessens.

Often I take God's sacrifice for us for granted. I forget that each day we have here is a precious, undeserved gift. I fail to remember that whatever happens to me today or tomorrow has less significance in the grand scheme of things, because my home in heaven is already secured. Today, as you complete your responsibilities and support your officer and live your normal routine, I urge you to take an extra moment to remember the sacrifice Jesus made on the cross for us and how that has forever changed our destinies.

PRAYER

Lord, I am constantly blown away by You. Your generosity, Your love, Your selflessness, Your grace, Your kindness. You have loved us with a love so deep that it is unfathomable. You sent Your Son to die for us. Even as we stumble and sin, You call us Your precious children. Forgive me, Lord, for not remembering this sacrifice enough. Forgive me for the days I take for granted. Let me always think of the love You have shown for us, and let me and my family live in a way that shares this with others.

DAY 40

WE WILL NOT GIVE UP

"But as for you, be strong and do not give up, for your work will be rewarded."
2 CHRONICLES 15:7

Let us not become weary in doing good, for at the proper time we will reap a harvest if we do not give up.
GALATIANS 6:9

The LORD directs the steps of the godly. He delights in every detail of their lives. Though they stumble, they will never fall, for the Lord holds them by the hand.
PSALM 37:23–24 NLT

I don't know about you, but there have been times in this blue life when I've wanted to give up. I've gotten sick of the shift work and just wanted to have a "normal" nine-to-five for my officer and me. I've gotten tired of rearranging holidays and celebrating special days early or late. I've gotten discouraged hearing of yet another family losing their hero and wanted to beg my officer to hang up his duty belt. Blue life is tough and demanding, and it comes with a lot of sacrifice and trials.

We're not alone in our thoughts of surrender. Throughout the Bible we read about a myriad of people who could have given up but didn't. Can you imagine how different things would look if Mary said, "Nah, I can't have this baby!" or if David was like, "This is too much. I'm out!" Or think about someone in your own life who could have given up on you but didn't. Think about how different things would be now. Think about how hard academy was for your officer and your family, and how easy it would have been to toss in the towel. There are so many aspects of blue life that tempt me to throw my hands up and say, "I quit!"

But we were not created to be quitters. We weren't created to give in to these trials. We may stumble and struggle, but we will not fall when we turn to the Lord for support. One of my absolute favorite verses of all time (yes, all time!) is Galatians 6:9. Because we can't see the final chapter (or sometimes even the road ahead of us), it can be hard to keep going, especially when we're not seeing the fruits of our labor.

I often think about our officers and the little thanks they receive for their hard work and sacrifice. Can you imagine if they decided to quit after a full shift during which no one was grateful? We wouldn't have any officers left! But thanked or not, they put on their uniform each day and go out to serve their communities. Thanked or not, you support them and love them.

Take heart, friend, for you and your officer *will* reap the benefits of your hard work and sacrifice. Keep going, be strong, lean on the Lord, and don't give up.

PRAYER

Lord, sometimes I am so tempted to give up. Sometimes the discouragement my officer and I face seems too hard to bear. Wrap your arms around us in these times, Lord, and lift us back onto our feet. Remind us of Your divine plan. Encourage us in a way that only You can. We know there is good for all who work toward Your plan, God. Help us fixate on this truth in times when we so desperately want to back down.

DAY 41

BEING GRATEFUL

Rejoice always, pray continually, give thanks in all circumstances; for this is God's will for you in Christ Jesus.
1 THESSALONIANS 5:16–18

I will give thanks to you, Lord, with all my heart; I will tell of all your wonderful deeds.
PSALM 9:1

"We give thanks to you, Lord God Almighty, who is and who was, for you have taken your great power and begun to reign."
REVELATION 11:17

Every year when November rolls around, we're reminded of how important it is to be grateful. We see thankful Thanksgiving posts left and right, and cute "Grateful" décor all over Pinterest. I love it all—but isn't it funny how we only really focus on gratefulness for one month each year? What if, instead, we enacted an attitude of gratitude in our daily life year-round?

My officer and I have a list hanging on our fridge with spots to write what we're thankful for in each other. Some days it's my making his lunch, some days it's his taking out the trash, and sometimes it's just a funny quirk or personality trait about the other that we enjoy. I regularly text my sister-in-law about things I'm grateful for. There's a section in my planner that has a spot for gratitude each week. And friends, all of this has been a game changer for my officer and me—personally and in our marriage.

Focusing on what we're thankful for makes a difference because it shifts our mindset. Instead of focusing on what we're lacking or what we want to change, we spend time counting our blessings and recounting the things we do have. Making an intentional shift to this changes our mindset, and praising God for those things shapes our hearts.

Throughout the Bible we're reminded to give thanks. We're told to praise Him for His good works, to sing of His praises, and to give thanks to heaven. When we take moments throughout the day to marinate on what we're grateful for and thank the Lord for those things, it instills the attitude of gratitude in our minds and souls.

Today I encourage you to spend some time writing down things for which you're thankful. Tell your officer something you're grateful for that he does. Text a friend something you love about them. Spend some time reveling in the blessings you've been given, instead of being swept up in what you're missing. Ask God to open your eyes to the positives in your life, and I promise you'll start to feel your heart and attitude change.

PRAYER

Lord, thank you for the constant blessings You rain down on my life. Even in the trials and dark times, You provide. Thank you for my health, my family, my home, and the safety of my officer. Help me remain in constant prayer with You, and open my eyes to all the blessings I have in my life. Help me see all that I am thankful for and focus on those things. Let our home be one overflowing with gratefulness, Lord, and let our life glorify You.

DAY 42

WE WILL WALK THROUGH IT TOGETHER

"Where you go I will go, and where you stay I will stay."
RUTH 1:16

I appeal to you, brothers and sisters, in the name of our Lord Jesus Christ, that all of you agree with one another in what you say and that there be no divisions among you, but that you be perfectly united in mind and thought.
1 CORINTHIANS 1:10

When my officer and I were teenagers, we'd often walk together along the country roads by his parents' house. I'd read somewhere (probably *Seventeen* magazine) that "the couple that walks together, stays together." We began walking together in high school and now, more than a decade later, we still walk our neighborhood together. We literally and figuratively walk hand in hand together through life. Through the valleys and up the mountains. We wait together in front of shut doors, we open new doors together, we take detours, and sometimes we have to go the long way, but through all of it we go together. What a beautiful thing God has given us—this privilege of getting to do life together with someone. What a blessing it is being able to walk side by side with our partner through the triumphs and trials of life.

Sometimes I think about all of this when we go on short strolls—just a quick jaunt around our neighborhood. I look at the man who was once a boy who has consistently loved me throughout the years. I look down at our clasped hands —the same hands that have graduated high school and college and grad school and academy, that have wiped away tears and started new careers, that have slid on wedding rings and have signed mortgage papers—and my heart explodes.

What a gift God gave us when He blessed us with our spouse. He did not create us to travel through life alone, but side by side with our officer and with Him as our travel guide. Life is full of ups and downs, and blue life is even more challenging. It isn't always easy, but it's always easier when we're hand in hand.

PRAYER

Lord, I am blown away by how much you have blessed me with the partnership my officer and I have. Thank you for creating someone to walk through life with, through both the trials and triumphs. This week I pray that You help us focus on strengthening our partnership and marriage. Help us take a moment to reflect on how far we've come as a team. Let our full hands be a reminder of the goodness You have promised to us and what You have already fulfilled.

DAY 43

THE ONE WHO WATCHES OVER YOU DOES NOT SLUMBER

I look to the mountains—does my help come from there? My help comes from the LORD, who made heaven and earth. He will not let you stumble, the one who watches over you will not slumber. Indeed, he who watches over Israel never slumbers or sleeps. The LORD himself watches over you. The LORD stands beside you as your protective shade. The sun will not harm you by day, nor the moon at night. The LORD keeps you from all harm and watches over your life. The LORD keeps watch over you as you come and go, both now and forever.

PSALM 121:1–8 NLT

"Do you not know? Have you not heard? The LORD is the everlasting God, the Creator of the ends of the earth. He will not grow tired or weary, and his understanding no one can fathom. He gives strength to the weary and increases the power of the weak."

ISAIAH 40:28–29

I used to have the hardest time sleeping when my officer first began working graves. Every little creak made my hair stand on end and each car that drove by caused me to stir. I would lie in bed, wide awake, worrying about my officer and about my safety. Would something happen to him? What if someone broke into our house? What if he was in an accident? What if our home caught fire? The thoughts ran back and forth through my mind when I should've been deep in sleep.

One day during my morning devo, I came across Psalm 121. The third line jumped off the pages and I read it over and over again. "He who watches over Israel will neither sleep nor slumber" (v. 3 NIV). As I repeatedly read that psalm, my nerves calmed. I felt a sense of peace about sleeping alone while my officer was out paroling the darkness—because even as I am snoozing, God is not.

God takes no days off. He doesn't take breaks from watching over us, and He's never napping when we cry out to Him. What a wonderful thing, to be able to call on someone who's always there for us.

As you lie down tonight or send your officer out the door, remember that the One who holds the world is also holding you. Remember that the mightiest of all is watching over your officer and your home, and let that bring comfort to your body and your mind.

PRAYER

Lord, thank you for always being here. You are my watcher, my protector, my helper—now and forever. Even when I'm feeling overwhelmed, You are here. Even when I feel like I'm falling short, You are calling me whole. Even when I feel lost, You are reminding me of Your plan. Thank you, God, for your constant love and guidance. Remind me of Your infinity when I'm straying. Remind me to breathe when I'm feeling breathless. You are always here, Lord, and for that I'm forever grateful.

DAY 44

IT TAKES A VILLAGE

Carry each other's burdens, and in this way you will fulfill the law of Christ.

GALATIANS 6:2

Most important of all, continue to show deep love for each other, for love covers a multitude of sins. Cheerfully share your home with those who need a meal or a place to stay. God has given each of you a gift from his great variety of spiritual gifts. Use them well to serve one another.

1 PETER 4:8–10 NLT

All the believers were together and had everything in common. They sold property and possessions to give to anyone who had need. Every day they continued to meet together in the temple courts. They broke bread in their homes and ate together with glad and sincere hearts, praising God and enjoying the favor of all the people. And the Lord added to their number daily those who were being saved.

ACTS 2:44–47

You know that old saying "it takes a village"? It's so true, and it's even more true when it comes to blue life. Having a law enforcement officer in the family changes the dynamic of pretty much...everything. Your schedule is distinct from most others, the way you celebrate holidays varies, what you consider "the weekend" is different, and the amount you worry and stress is through the roof. And because you're a police wife, I know you're good at being independent, because you have to be. But that doesn't mean that you can't ask for help and turn to others for support.

Why is it that it's so hard to ask for help sometimes? Maybe it's our pride, or that we don't want to be a burden to someone else. Maybe it's our worry that we'll be seen as weak or incompetent. There is a million different reasons that can stop us for reaching out. Reach out anyway.

Ask your neighbor for that cup of sugar when you don't have time to run to the store. Ask your friend out for lunch on a day you're craving some burgers and fellowship. Take your mom up on her offer to watch the kids for the evening. Simply say thank you when your uncle offers to rotate your tires instead of arguing that you can take it in yourself. And in turn, extend that hospitality and friendship to the others in your life. There's a reason why connecting with other police wives is encouraged in blogs and in books—because this life is hard, and we're not meant to go through it alone.

We were created for relationship, and I believe God is happiest when He sees us serving one another in love. Today I urge you to put aside your pride and take up that old friend on their offer to treat you to coffee, or to ask your dad to help you finish that painting project you've been meaning to finally get done for the past six months. Asking for or receiving help is not weak or selfish. When we use the village around us to help support us, our officers, and our families, we're happier and less stressed, and enjoying the company that God intended us to have. How will you reach out to your village today?

PRAYER

Lord, You know that sometimes my pride gets in the way and I struggle to reach out for help. Rid my heart of that pride, God, and remind me that You have created us for community. Let me receive assistance joyfully and gratefully, and let me give it just as gladly. Help my family connect with others who will bring us closer to You. Lead us to those who we can be in fellowship with, serving one another as You would.

DAY 45

MORNING MUSTER

"But when you pray, go away by yourself, shut the door behind you, and pray to your Father in private. Then your Father, who sees everything, will reward you."
MATTHEW 6:6 NLT

Look to the LORD and his strength; seek his face always.
1 CHRONICLES 16:11

Very early in the morning, while it was still dark, Jesus got up, left the house and went off to a solitary place, where he prayed.
MARK 1:35

At the beginning of each shift, my officer attends muster with the other cops on his squad. It's a time to check in with each other and the shifts before them, make sure everyone is on the same page, share updates, and also spend time in community with one another before a soon-to-be-busy shift. It's a way to prioritize things and get into the mindset the day requires. Isn't this similar to what we should be doing every morning with God?

I'll be the first to admit that I'm not perfect about this. I would love to say that I have my quiet time each and every morning without fail, but the truth is, some days it simply doesn't happen. Sometimes I sleep in, get sidetracked, or maybe even rush through it. When those mornings happen, I notice a big difference in the way the rest of my day goes. If I spend the first chunk of my day scrolling social media, I'm more likely to be scattered throughout the day, and quicker to anger and rush to judgement. If I spend it with Jesus, I'm more likely to be intentional and calm, and feel God's presence in my life. When I root myself in the Word each morning, it dictates how the rest of my day will go.

The world is really good at pulling us in a million different directions. There's so many things biding for our attention—our jobs, our families, our interests—and if we're not careful we can easily get swept away in a combination of any of those things. Just as muster sets the pace for our officer's shift, having quiet time with Jesus spent in Scripture and prayer sets the pace for the rest of our day.

PRAYER

Lord, thank you for this time I get with You. Help me make my devotional time a priority. Even though there's a million things I "need" to do, spending time with You in Your Word is the most important. I ask for You to show up today and make Your presence known. Let me rest in Your embrace and feel calmed by

Your companionship. As I build the foundation of my week and my life, let me always make sure that You are the rock on which it sits.

DAY 46

LIVING A LIFE THAT POINTS TO JESUS

He said to them, "Go into all the world and preach the gospel to all creation."

MARK 16:15

"You are the light of the world. A town built on a hill cannot be hidden. Neither do people light a lamp and put it under a bowl. Instead they put it on its stand, and it gives light to everyone in the house. In the same way, let your light shine before others, that they may see your good deeds and glorify your Father in heaven."

MATTHEW 5:14–17

In everything set them an example by doing what is good. In your teaching show integrity, seriousness and soundness of speech that cannot be condemned, so that those who oppose you may be ashamed because they have nothing bad to say about us.

TITUS 2:7–8

There are reminders all around our house of my officer's profession. Some are easier to recognize, like the patrol car in the driveway and the thin blue line flag on the wall. Some things are harder to spot. You need to open the closet door to see the row of hanging uniforms, or go into the office to see the cop caddy sitting in the corner. If you dig through the laundry you're bound to find a couple of stray bullets, and if you step into the garage you'll notice a pair of dirty range boots kicked off at the steps. Between the obvious and the more secluded things, there are hints of blue life everywhere around our home.

If you were to take stock on your life in the same way, would you see God's presence there? I'm not necessarily talking about the Bible sitting on your nightstand or the Scripture on your wall. I'm talking about the way you speak to your children, the way you treasure your spouse, and the overall way you live your life. Are you slow to anger or quick to correct? Are you gentle when leading your kids, or harsh and impatient? Are you managing your finances and tithing, or are you sinking deeper in debt and spending carelessly? Are you able to forgive, or are you holding on to resentment and blame?

More people are led to Jesus by observing actions, not hearing words. We are called to live a life that glorifies God. We are to treat others as Christ treated us—which, of course, is much easier said than done. Just as it's easy for us to spot our officer's things around our home, let it be easy for others to see Jesus in us. Let it be obvious that our home serves the Lord, and let our actions point others back to Him.

PRAYER

Lord, I pray that when others look around at my life, they see You there. When I answer someone's request for advice, let it be rooted in Your Word. When I'm slow to anger, let people see it's because of You. As I bow my head before our meal, let them see what You have blessed us with. Let it be obvious that You are the captain of my life, and let Your hand rest on all that is precious to me. Let me lead a life that points to you, God.

DAY 47

THE LORD DETERMINES OUR PATHS

We can make our plans, but the LORD determines our steps.
PROVERBS 16:9 NLT

We may throw the dice, but the LORD determines how they fall.
PROVERBS 16:33 NLT

Trust in the LORD with all of your heart and lean not on your own understanding; in all your ways submit to him, and he will make your paths straight.
PROVERBS 3:5–6

I'm a planner. I always have been. I like knowing what to expect and am not a fan of surprises. You can imagine, then, how blue life turned my life upside down at first!

If there's one thing that all police wives become rock stars at, it's being flexible. Our officers' schedules are constantly changing, and it's a small miracle each time they actually walk through the front door on time. I quickly realized (while my officer was still in academy) that my stick-to-the-plan attitude was not going to bode well with our new lifestyle. As the months of FTO passed, we became even better at this, as every few weeks my officer's schedule would change. Different shifts, different days, different sergeants. It truly seemed like every day was completely different from the last!

And as time went on, I realized that I didn't mind as much anymore. Sure, I still hated when I had to scrape my officer's dinner from his plate to a Tupperware container because he got stuck at work again, but it didn't cause me the same annoyance that it used to. I still worried each night as I climbed into bed alone, hoping my officer was okay as he battled what lurks out there in the dark, but I didn't have the same anxiety and overwhelming fear that I used to.

In Proverbs we're told that regardless of how we plan or how we throw the dice, it's God who will determine our outcome. It's not us who makes the plans; it's Him. And His plans are perfect. I'm not yet where I strive to be, but I'm way more flexible and trusting than I used to be, thanks to this chaotic blue life.

PRAYER

Lord, You are all-knowing. Thank you for having the perfect plan for me and my family. You have named and numbered the stars and know each strand of hair on my head. Forgive me for thinking that I know better than You. Forgive me for not trusting You enough to hand over the reins. Help me surrender to You, Lord, for Your plans are good. Help me trust Your path, even when I cannot see the end.

DAY 48

COMPARISON IS A THIEF

A heart at peace gives life to the body, but envy rots the bones.
PROVERBS 14:30

Am I now trying to win the approval of human beings, or of God? Or am I trying to please people? If I were still trying to please people, I would not be a servant of Christ.
GALATIANS 1:10

Do nothing out of selfish ambition or vain conceit. Rather, in humility value others above yourselves.
PHILIPPIANS 2:3

I think we as humans have always had a problem with comparing ourselves to others, but lately, with the addition of technology and social media, everything seems amplified. It's become incredibly easy to see our high-school classmate's promotion or our cousin's fancy new car, because it's in high-def on the screen right in front of us. Or maybe it's not what's online, but what we hear about—like the LEOW's upgraded wedding band her officer got her or your officer's coworker's promotion to lieutenant. We can also stumble into thinking that we're better than others. Maybe we glance at an unflattering photo and think, *I can't believe she posted that!* or maybe we see an old friend graduating from community college and think, *About time! I've had my degree for years now.*

Teddy Roosevelt once said that comparison is the thief of joy. I think that it's the thief pretty much anything and everything precious to us. It robs us of our joy, yes, but it also robs us of our time. How often do we sit on our couch, scrolling through social media, wishing for this girl's outfit or that family's vacation? It robs us of our patience. We want this car or that house right now. It robs us of the contentment with what we already have. Our marriages suddenly seem less, our jobs seem less, and our unmanicured lawns seem less.

I have to work diligently to keep my desire to compare in check. I have to keep tabs on my jealous side and take steps to intentionally squash it down into the ground where it belongs. The truth is, social media is a highlight reel, not real life. We can't compare our lows to someone else's highs, just like we can't look at someone's winning season and think that they've never had a losing season. When you feel that tug to compare, think of three things you're grateful for instead. In lieu of coveting that Caribbean vacation your coworker is on, remember a fond family memory or precious moment with your spouse.

PRAYER

Lord, You know I struggle with comparison. Help me to value others above myself while not losing sight of my own worth. Stop me from scrolling when it harms me, and rid me of my jealous thoughts. Let me be pleased for others when they see success, and pleased for my family each time we see success ourselves. Help me replace my envious thoughts with thoughts of gratefulness and contentedness.

DAY 49

IT'S OKAY TO NOT BE OK

Hear my cry, O God, listen to my prayer. From the end of the earth I call to you, I call as my heart grows faint; lead me to the rock that is higher than I. For you have been my refuge, a strong tower against the foe. I long to dwell in your tent forever and take refuge in the shelter of your wings.

Psalm 61:1–4

Cast all your anxiety on him because he cares for you.

1 Peter 5:7

He was despised and rejected by mankind, a man of suffering, and familiar with pain. Like one from whom people hide their faces he was despised, and we held him in low esteem.

Isaiah 53:3

I know you're strong, because you're a police wife. I know that most of the time you're really good at keeping it all together and putting on a happy face for your officer and your family. You're amazing—there's no denying that! But I'm here to tell you that sometimes it's okay to not be okay, and that you don't have to feel guilty or ashamed about those "down days."

When thinking about the people in the Bible who have also struggled, I remember David. Through his beautiful psalms he shared his trials of anguish, loneliness, and despair. Even Jesus himself was familiar with pain. He went through trials and suffering. Some of the strongest and most faithful people had times of extreme sadness—so don't you think it's believable, then, that we would feel this way sometimes too?

We're not asked to have it all together, or to be upbeat 100 percent of the time. Times of doubt or depression do not equal ungratefulness or a lack of faith, regardless of what our culture may tell us. Some mornings you might need to roll over and spend some extra time snuggled in bed or to stop and get a large frothy latte on the way to work. Maybe your self-care looks like a steamy bubble bath and that book you've been meaning to crack open. Or maybe it just looks like sitting in your car an extra five minutes while listening to your worship playlist before rushing off to your next responsibility. Whatever that self-care looks like, I encourage you to take some extra moments for yourself today. Spend some extra time in prayer, sing along to your favorite worship song, and do one thing that's just for you—because you're absolutely worth it. What will it be?

PRAYER

Lord, today is one of those days. Be present with me as I struggle through my day. Pick me up as I'm feeling down. Let me feel Your arms around me, and remind me of Your steady comfort. Let me not feel guilty for taking some time for myself. You have created me in Your image and You want me to take care of myself. Help me prioritize my self-care this week as I reach out to You.

DAY 50

JUST LOVE

Above all, love each other deeply, because love covers a multitude of sins.

1 PETER 4:8

If I speak in the tongues of men or of angels, but do not have love, I am only a resounding gong or a clanging cymbal. If I have the gift of prophecy and can fathom all mysteries and all knowledge, and if I have a faith that can move mountains, but do not have love, I am nothing. If I give all I possess to the poor and give over my body to hardship that I may boast, but do not have love, I gain nothing.

1 CORINTHIANS 13:1–3

Our life is messy and our marriage isn't perfect. I'm always finding stray bullets and belt keepers around the house, I get frustrated at my officer's schedule, I forget to pick up the main ingredient to make dinner, and I have a laundry basket that's constantly overflowing. Our life is messy, but I love it that way. Our marriage isn't perfect, but it's perfect for us. That's because of love, friends. Our love for each other, our love for our God, our love for our home, and our love for our life. There are a million things that could be going better or differently and a million more things on my to-do list, but as long as we're loving 110 percent, I think we're doing okay.

We can get so caught up in making sure that our house looks a certain way, that our car is the latest model, that we're on time for each and every activity on our kid's schedule, and that we look the part at church. As followers of Christ we're called to do a lot of things, but the most important thing is just to love.

Your kids don't care about their perfectly packed lunch as much as they care about the nights you snuggle in bed with them and stretch out their bedtime story. Your officer doesn't care about his uniform being pressed and cleaned when he opens the closet as much as you being there with open arms when he gets home after a rough shift. Those neighbors who haven't yet accepted Christ into their life don't care that you can recite one hundred Bible verses as much as they notice you being patient and kind and generous in the way that you love them and the others on the block.

There's always going to be another blue family who looks like they all have it together. There's always going to be things on your to-do list. There's always going to be responsibilities at church, at work, and at home. But as you wade through life, navigating this blue chaos, I pray you remember that as long as you're loving on people, you're doing it right.

PRAYER

Lord, I know You have a calling for me and my family and expectations for us as Your children. I also know that above all else You have called us to love one another and to love You. Remind me of how important this is when I'm busy. Remind me of this when I'm distracted. Remind me of this when I get swept up in other things. You are the greatest example of love that we have. Let my actions resemble Yours as I share Your love with others and love them in the way that You would.

NOTES

Day 22

1. "Corrie ten Boom > Quotes > Quotable Quotes," *Goodreads*, https://www.goodreads.com/quotes/254564-there-is-no-pit-so-deep-that-god-s-love-is.

ABOUT THE AUTHOR

Cote is the face behind the faith based police wife blog ammo+grace. She is an active presence in the law enforcement community on various social media platforms, sharing her experience with fellow LEOWs and blue supporters through relatable photos and impactful words. Cote lives in the Pacific Northwest with her husband, who is a city police officer and her high school sweetheart. This book is her debut as a published author.

CPSIA information can be obtained
at www.ICGtesting.com
Printed in the USA
BVHW041000151019
561050BV00022BA/1034/P